Wok
For Less

For all my wokstars, this book is for you.
May your kitchen table be always full of love
and joy. Keep shining and wok on.

Wok

Ching-He Huang

Photography by Jamie Cho

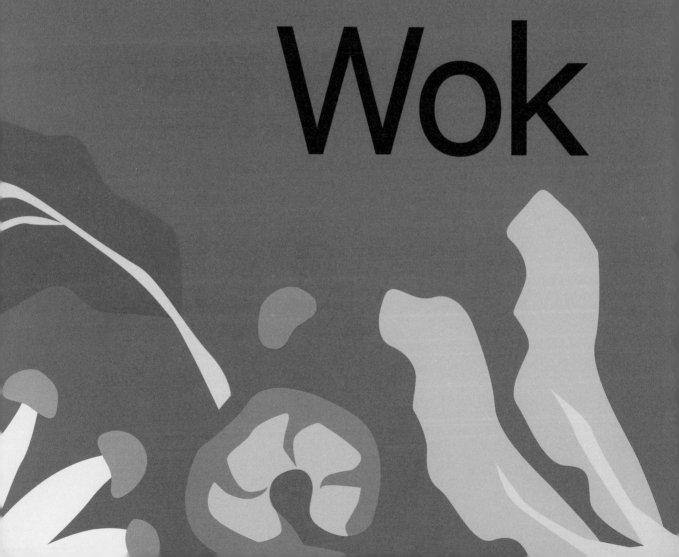

Budget-Friendly
Asian Meals in 30 Minutes
or Less

For Less

KYLE BOOKS

An Hachette UK Company
www.hachette.co.uk

First published in Great Britain in 2024 by
Kyle Books, an imprint of Octopus Publishing Group Limited
Carmelite House
50 Victoria Embankment
London EC4Y 0DZ
www.octopusbooks.co.uk

ISBN: 9781804191590

Distributed in the US by Hachette Book Group, 1290 Avenue of the Americas,
4th and 5th Floors, New York, NY 10104

Distributed in Canada by Canadian Manda Group, 664 Annette St.,
Toronto, Ontario, Canada M6S 2C8

Publishing Director: Judith Hannam
Publisher: Joanna Copestick
Editorial Assistant: Emma Hanson
Design: Evi O. Studio | Katherine Zhang & Emi Chiba
Photography: Jamie Cho
Food Styling and Props: Ching-He Huang
Production: Emily Noto

Printed and bound in China

10 9 8 7 6 5 4 3 2 1

Introduction

As I write this book, the cost of living crisis is at an all-time high. Never before has the cost of energy and food been this astronomical. Speedy, nutritious meals on a budget have become a necessity and I hope this book will help you to achieve that. Despite the dark clouds circulating the economy, I hope this book will blow away some of the blues, so that you find joy and comfort in these recipes. I hope that you will glean new ideas and tips, whether you are a meat lover or veggie, I hope there is something here for you and your loved ones. Lots of love, Ching xx

Pared-Down pantry

It is certainly true that Asian cooking has always been rather economical: a small dash and splash here and there using store-cupboard ingredients allow you to create maximum flavours at minimum cost. However, with the increasing need to curb spending on those non-essentials, I've designed this book in such a way that with an investment of around £50 or less you can build your pared-down pantry, which will allow you to use these store-cupboard necessities time and time again, so you can focus on buying fresh and sometimes canned ingredients. You can build up the pantry as you go – concentrate on a handful of essentials from the recipes that interest or excite you, then keep adding to your pantry and repertoire as you work your way through the book.

A Note of Advice

Not all sauces are created equal, as some have been fermented for longer, some have less or more sodium. Find sauces that are rich in umami so you need even less of each condiment for maximum flavour. These are my pared-down Asian pantry ingredients:

Storecupboard

Low-sodium light soy sauce or tamari

Dark soy sauce

Shaohsing rice wine or mirin

Hoisin sauce

Oyster sauce or vegetarian mushroom sauce

Chilli bean sauce

Black bean sauce

Toasted sesame oil

Clear rice vinegar

Miso sauce

Fresh flavourings

Garlic

Ginger

Chillies

Coriander

Spring onions

Red onions or shallots

White onions

For cooking

Rapeseed oil or coconut oil

Western store-cupboard

Olive oil

Honey, golden syrup or sugar

Vegetable bouillon powder

Salt

Ground black pepper

Ground white pepper

Peanut butter

Spices

Chinese five spice

Dried chilli flakes

Ground cumin

Fennel seeds

Sichuan peppercorns

Rice

Jasmine rice, brown or basmati rice

Noodles

Udon noodles

Ramen noodles

Egg noodles

Vermicelli rice noodles

Wonton skins or dumpling skins

Nuts and seeds

Black sesame seeds

White sesame seeds

Cashew nuts

Walnuts

Almonds

Note If you are gluten intolerant use gluten-free options or substitutes where possible

No Deep-Frying

The foundation of Chinese and Asian cooking relies on the trusted wok and the main style of cooking is stir-fried, which in itself is a very economical way of cooking. Cooking very quickly over a concentrated high heat using the smallest amount of fuel will save you more money than using the oven for slow cooking. Of course, cooking is about variety and so if you cook predominantly stir-fries, then the 'Budget Chop Suey, Stir-Fries & Fried Rice' chapter (see page 16) in particular will help you to combine ingredients. Most of the recipes in this book do not involve deep-frying, to reduce both fuel usage and cooking oil. The only exception is the Shanghainese Lionhead Pork Meatball Noodle Soup recipe (see page 175). Deep-frying is not particularly healthy, so it is best to avoid it entirely if you can and stick to stir-frying, steaming, boiling or oven cooking – in that order.

Roasting

Roasting is an easy way to cook for a large crowd and I have included some dishes that require the use of the oven, but you could also use an air fryer if you have one. My advice is to just use what you have, rather than spending on further equipment. To make the most of the heat and space in the oven, plan ahead and roast some extra food, for example some extra chicken thighs or char siu (Chinese roast pork), on another shelf at the same time. This way you get the most out of the space in the oven, and you can repurpose the extra food to use the next day. Planning is key and goes hand in hand with budgeting meals.

Easy Freeze-able options

The 'Easy Freezy' chapter (see page 160) looks at making your own dumplings, wontons, siu mai, fish balls, prawn balls and meatballs, which you can freeze and then cook from frozen. Plus I always have some frozen seafood like squid, prawns and mussels as well as frozen peas, which are super handy for making fried rice, wontons and dumplings. Frozen ramen noodles, bao buns and, of course, not forgetting fried tofu are also often in my freezer for those emergency suppers. I love buying from alternative stores and not just from the supermarket, but larger Chinese supermarkets tend to buy in bulk and so are often cheaper; check them out if you are after something like a large sack of rice, bundles of noodles or frozen seafood.

Minimal Equipment

Most of the recipes in this book rely on a good, flat-bottom wok – it could be seasoned carbon steel or unseasoned carbon steel. These days my go-tos are my trusted Lotus wok together with my John Lewis stainless steel wok: they're low maintenance and reliable – like good old friends. But don't go spending on a shiny new one, just use whatever you have. And if you don't have a wok, a pan will do.

For cutting I mostly use my Chinese cleaver or chef's all-purpose knife, plus a chopping board and a bamboo steamer that sits on my wok – a stainless-steel steaming rack that fits on the wok also works great. I find a garlic press handy, for speed and to save on chopping; a microplane or grater for ginger; plus a good food processor to make fish balls or meatballs, which is incredibly efficient. All these help to make meal prep effortless. A specific non-stick crêpe pan will help to make the Taiwanese Lun Piah pancake (see page 54), but that is probably the exception. Of course, some pots and pans are a must; again, use what you have without the need to buy any new or expensive equipment.

Cook's Notes

Before you 'wok on', there are just a few cook's notes I would love to share with you.

Shop Wise

Substitute where you can. This book is designed for all, whether you are a meat lover or plant based, and Asian cuisine lends itself to flexitarian diets. It's pretty easy to swap out ingredients, so where possible, I have suggested substitutes. I want you to make these recipes your own, so if a dish calls for cauliflower but you only have broccoli, use that instead. Everything is interchangeable.

Aside from a handful of specific Asian ingredients, all the ingredients used in this book can be found in mainstream supermarkets, and you may add them to your shopping basket on a weekly basis anyway, so it should be effortlessly easy. If you shop at a farmers' market, or are trying to grow your own foods, then having access to seasonal produce is even better for interchanging ingredients. Plus you can come up with various creative options, which is always satisfying when they work, keeping cooking fun.

Go Nuts

I use a handful of types of seeds and nuts in this book. From black sesame seeds and white sesame seeds, to cashew nuts, almonds and walnuts, they all add texture and nutrition and give a satisfying fuller feeling to the meals. I buy unsalted nuts and seeds in bulk and roast the nuts in the oven for 6 minutes at 180°C (350°F), Gas Mark 4. You can store them in jars (cool the nuts first) and they are so handy to pop into your dishes. It really pays to shop around, as there are various health food stores and local Asian superstores where buying in bulk is more economical.

Fruit Platter for Dessert

The Asian dessert is usually a plate of fresh fruit at the end of the meal, perhaps some slices of apple, chunks of pineapple or orange segments (usually served at Chinese restaurants). Eating in this way helps digestion, is better for overall health and since the whole fruit is eaten (not juiced), you get the fibre. Plus it won't spike your blood sugar, since it's eaten at the end of the meal. Eating too many sugar-laden desserts doesn't help anyone; they contain empty calories and have very little nutritional benefits, which are especially important when you are trying to eat healthy. But by cutting them out, you're saving money as well as your health. Of course no one is a saint, so the occasional treat is fine, just try to prioritize fruit over sugary desserts most of the time to maintain this healthy habit.

Menu Planner

Two-Meal Wonders

Similar ingredients for consecutive meals.

Spicy Cumin Lamb (see page 156)

Spicy Cumin Lamb & Pea Fried Rice
(see page 159)

Roast Chilli Chicken (see page 128)

Roast Chicken Fried Rice (see page 130)

Honey Soy Chicken x Mangetout x Walnuts
(see page 28)

Chicken Pad Thai with Crunchy Veggie
Noodles (see page 82)

Saucy Oyster Sauce Beef & Broccoli Chow
Mein (see page 86)

Japanese Teriyaki Beef Udon Noodle Stir-Fry
(see page 88)

Bang Bang Chicken Peanut Noodles
(see page 84)

Spicy Peanut Noodles (see page 76)

Buddha's Chow Mein (see page 71)

Spicy Mushroom Egg Noodles (see page 72)

Shanghainese-Style Mini 'Cloud' Wonton
Noodle Soup (see page 66)

Chicken & Sweetcorn Egg-Drop Wonton Skin
Soup (see page 56)

Egg & Tomato Spring Onion Scramble
(see page 48)

Cantonese-Style Ham & Egg Fried Rice
(see page 30)

A Little Goes a Long Way

Using diced meat, offcuts or leftover ingredients.

On a Budget

Fried rice makes all things nice.

1.

Budget Chop Suey, Stir-Fries & Fried Rice

1 Budget Chop Suey, Stir-Fries & Fried Rice

This chapter is all about using up odds and ends that you may have in the refrigerator to create delicious budget meals; it is super versatile.

This chapter is a nod to chop suey, a 'hash' that American Chinese restauranteurs created for the Western palate. It is also known as 'za sui' in Mandarin, and traditionally uses up entrails and offal in a kind of stew. The Americanized Chinese versions were often a mix of vegetables, meat or seafood in a brown gravy sauce.

This chapter is inspired by this concept – but instead of having a saucy gravy, my dishes are a drier type of stir-fry, keeping the ingredients to a minimum.

You can double the quantities to serve two or they can be a large meal for one: my portions err on the generous side. You can use whatever leftover ingredients you have in the refrigerator.

These dishes could be served as a quick lunch if you are working from home or as a quick mid-week supper. Minimal prep time is key, as is, of course, a minimum budget, while they're also big on taste. It's amazing how a little handful of ingredients can be worked together to make a delicious meal.

For vegan friends, I have included straightforward ingredient substitutes that will work quite well in the recipes. Throughout the book, you are welcome to use tofu (fried, smoked, firm, soft), tempeh, seitan, mushrooms and beans like edamame and chickpeas as substitutes if you like, or you can just bulk up on the veggies.

There are dishes like my Bacon x French Beans x Peanuts stir-fry (see page 32); Ham x Peas x Spring Onion (see page 39); Smoked Tofu x Veggie Stir-Fry x Cashew Nuts (see page 20); 'Everything' Chop Suey (see page 40); Honey Soy Chicken x Mangetout x Walnuts (see page 28); spicy Sichuan Pork x Cucumber x Chilli Sauce (see page 34). These are just some classics to have in your repertoire. To make the meals super speedy, I often have leftover jasmine rice, which can be reheated once more for a quick accompanying dish to mop up all the flavours.

It's not just chop suey dishes that are budget friendly but also trusty fried rice, and in this chapter I share with you my favourite go-to fried rice recipes. When I think about fried rice, I think about my paternal grandmother who owned several paddy fields. Harvesting rice was back-breaking work that started in the very cool early hours of the morning, before the heat become unbearable. She would scold anyone for wasting even one grain of rice, often comparing it to a bead of sweat in the sun.

To make the most use of the humble grain, you can experiment with many different types – brown, mixed grains, wild grains, red rice, black rice, etc.; they all have differing qualities and nutrients. If you feel flush, you can boost your pantry with these types of rice, which will be more nutritious than simple long-grain or basmati rice. I actually prefer jasmine rice from Thailand; it is aromatic and the perfect backdrop for mopping up flavourful dishes. It is not too expensive either, as I tend to reach for supermarkets' own brands.

The trick to cooking rice well is to wash the rice thoroughly. Do this in a sieve under cold running water until the water runs clear, which will get rid of any excess starch and prevent the grains becoming all claggy. Then cook it using the absorption method (see page 22), which is probably the easiest way. Before you attempt the recipes in this chapter, it will help to read through my tips for cooking with rice. Practice makes perfect and it does begin with the basics. Once mastered, you can do it with your eyes closed and make speedy dishes in a flash. All the recipes in this chapter call for already cooked jasmine rice, which you should have to hand. My advice for best results is to use leftover jasmine rice and dress with some toasted sesame oil to help separate and loosen the grains before you reheat.

In this chapter, the fried rice recipes include my Sweet Soy Smoked Tofu x Chickpea Fried Rice (see page 22); Five Spice Lardons x Red Cabbage Fried Rice (see page 36); Prawn x Edamame Fried Rice (see page 26); Cantonese-Style Ham Egg Fried Rice (see page 30) just to name a few. I hope you enjoy them.

10 mins

5 mins

Smoked Tofu x Veggie Stir-Fry x Cashew Nuts

Serves 1

1 tbsp rapeseed oil

1 garlic clove, peeled, crushed, and finely chopped

2.5cm (1in) piece of fresh root ginger, peeled and finely grated

1 red chilli, deseeded and finely chopped

½ red onion, sliced

100g (3½oz) smoked tofu, sliced into strips

1 tsp dark soy sauce

1 carrot, trimmed and sliced into julienne strips on the diagonal

½ red pepper, cored, deseeded and sliced into strips

2 spring onions, trimmed and sliced into 5cm (2in) pieces

1 tbsp Shaohsing rice wine

1 tbsp vegetarian mushroom sauce

1 tbsp low-sodium light soy sauce

1 tsp golden syrup

1 tsp toasted sesame oil

8 whole roasted, unsalted cashew nuts, halved

cooked jasmine rice (see page 22), to serve

black sesame seeds, to garnish

This is a great dish for clearing the refrigerator. It's amazing what a little carrot, red pepper and spring onion can do! Or you can use whatever veggies you have to hand – this one is delicious and versatile.

Heat a wok over a high heat until smoking. Add the rapeseed oil and give it a swirl. Add the garlic, ginger, red chilli and red onion and toss for a few seconds.

Add the smoked tofu and season with the dark soy sauce, then toss for a few seconds. Add the carrot, red pepper and spring onions, then season with Shaohsing rice wine.

Add the vegetarian mushroom sauce, light soy sauce and golden syrup and toss well. Season with the toasted sesame oil, then add the roasted cashew nuts. Sprinkle over the black sesame seeds and serve with jasmine rice.

Sweet Soy Smoked Tofu x Chickpea Fried Rice

Serves 2

1 tbsp rapeseed oil

2.5cm (1in) piece of fresh root ginger, peeled and very finely chopped

1 red chilli, deseeded and finely chopped

1 white onion, finely diced

½ × 420g (15oz) can chickpeas, drained and rinsed well

50g (1¾oz) block smoked tofu, finely cubed

1 tsp dark soy sauce

1 tbsp golden syrup

200g (7oz) cooked jasmine rice (see page 22)

1–2 tbsp low-sodium light soy sauce

dash of toasted sesame oil

pinch of ground white pepper

1 spring onion, trimmed and finely sliced, to garnish

This the perfect vegan dinner. I love the combination of chickpeas and smoked tofu wrapped in sweet, smoky soy flavours. If you want to bulk the dish up, add a pack of stir-fried vegetables before you add the rice, or you can simply have it on its own. It's definitely one of my favourite fried rice dishes.

Heat a wok over a medium heat until smoking. Add the rapeseed oil and give it a swirl. Add the ginger, red chilli and white onion and toss for a few seconds, then stir for another 20 seconds.

Add the chickpeas and smoked tofu pieces and stir together. Season with the dark soy sauce and golden syrup, then toss together well.

Add the cooked jasmine rice and, using a wooden spoon or metal spatula, start to gently break apart the rice grains by gently tossing and folding, for 1–2 minutes.

Add the light soy sauce and toss well to combine. Season with the toasted sesame oil and ground white pepper.

Garnish with spring onions and serve immediately.

Basic Jasmine Rice

Serves 4

350g (12oz) jasmine rice or basmati rice, washed until the water runs clear

600ml (20fl oz) filtered water

½–1 tbsp toasted sesame oil (optional, if frying – see tip opposite)

My top tip is to wash the rice well in a sieve under cold running water until the water runs clear. This will get rid of any excess starch and not make the grains all claggy. Then you can cook it using the absorption method below which is the easiest way. Practice makes perfect and, once you master it, you can do it with your eyes closed and make speedy dishes in a flash.

Place the rice in a heavy-based saucepan and add the water. Bring to the boil, uncovered, and then cover with a tight-fitting lid and reduce to a low heat. Cook for 15–20 minutes. Uncover the pan and remove from the heat. Fluff up the rice grains with a fork and serve immediately, or prepare for frying (see tip opposite).

Wok For Less

10 mins   5 mins

Smoked Tofu x Long-Stem Broccoli Fried Rice

Serves 2

1 tbsp rapeseed oil

1 garlic clove, finely chopped

2.5cm (1in) piece of fresh root ginger, peeled and very finely chopped

1 red chilli, deseeded and finely chopped

1 white onion, finely diced

1 handful of Tenderstem broccoli stalks, finely diced

1 tbsp Shaohsing rice wine or dry sherry

50g (1¾oz) block smoked tofu, finely cubed

½ tsp dark soy sauce

½ tsp chilli bean sauce

300g (10½oz) cooked jasmine rice (see page 22)

1–2 tbsp low-sodium light soy sauce

dash of toasted sesame oil

pinch of ground white pepper

Here the smoky tofu goes beautifully with the flavours of the rice wine, chilli bean sauce and soy sauce, and the tender broccoli stalks add crunch and bite – a marriage made in veggie heaven.

Heat a wok over a medium heat until smoking. Add the rapeseed oil and give it a swirl. Add the garlic, ginger, red chilli and white onion and toss for a few seconds, then stir-fry for 20 seconds.

Add the broccoli stalks and toss for 1 minute, adding the Shaohsing rice wine or sherry halfway through to help soften the broccoli stalks. Add the cubed smoked tofu pieces and stir together. Season with the dark soy sauce and chilli bean sauce, then toss together well.

Add the cooked jasmine rice and, using a wooden spoon or metal spatula, start to gently break apart the rice grains: not in a stabbing motion but by gently tossing and folding for 1–2 minutes.

Add the light soy sauce and toss well to combine. Season with the toasted sesame oil and ground white pepper and serve immediately.

Tip   If preparing for frying, immediately after making the freshly cooked rice, fan it out on a roasting tray to remove excess moisture. Place in the refrigerator uncovered and let it cool for 30 minutes. Remove from the refrigerator, drizzle over some toasted sesame oil and rub in-between the grains.

If you are making a fried rice dish using leftover rice that has already cooled in the refrigerator, then just drizzle over and rub in some toasted sesame oil before frying.

10 mins

5 mins

Prawns x Water Chestnuts x Onion x Peanuts

Serves 1

1 tbsp rapeseed oil

1 garlic clove, finely chopped

1 small red onion,
sliced into half-moons

6 large frozen tiger prawns,
defrosted, shelled, deveined
(or use cooked prawns)
and sliced in half or cubed,
or use frozen baby shrimp

1 tsp Shaohsing rice wine
or dry sherry

3–4 pieces whole canned water
chestnuts, drained

½ tsp chilli bean sauce or miso paste

1–2 tbsp low-sodium light soy sauce

6–8 roasted, unsalted peanuts

cooked rice, to serve

½ red chilli, sliced on a deep angle,
to garnish

Texture is king in this recipe – juicy tiger prawns are tossed in a spicy, umami chilli bean sauce. Crunchy water chestnuts add sweetness, the red onions add a bite and the peanuts add a deep savoury note. I love it when leftover ingredients come together like this – a total match made in heaven. Slice each whole prawn in half to make a little go a long way, or use frozen baby shrimp and cook straight from frozen.

Heat a wok over a high heat until smoking. Add the rapeseed oil and give it a swirl. Add the garlic and red onion and stir-fry for a few seconds, then add the tiger prawns. If using raw prawns or frozen baby shrimp, cook stirring for 1 minute, then add the Shaohsing rice wine or sherry. If using cooked prawns, add the Shaohsing rice wine immediately.

Add the water chestnuts and toss for 1 minute. Add the chilli bean sauce or miso, then season with the light soy sauce. Add the roasted, unsalted peanuts and give it one last toss. Serve with rice of your choice, garnished with the sliced chilli.

Prawn x Edamame Fried Rice

Serves 2

1 tbsp rapeseed oil

2 spring onions, trimmed and sliced into 1cm (½in) rounds, greens and whites separated

1 large handful of frozen edamame beans

8 tiger prawns, shelled, deveined and sliced in half down the middle

1 tbsp Shaohsing rice wine

½ tsp dark soy sauce

220g (7¾oz) cooked jasmine rice (see page 22)

1–2 tbsp low-sodium light soy sauce

dash of toasted sesame oil

pinch of ground white pepper

dried chilli flakes, to serve

I love the combination of the sweetness of the prawns, crunchiness of the edamame beans and bite of the spring onions. Slice the prawns in half to make it go a little further. This is great fried rice on a budget.

Heat a wok over a medium heat until smoking. Add the rapeseed oil and give it a swirl. Add the white parts of the spring onions. Toss for less than 20 seconds, then add the frozen edamame and toss for 10 seconds. Add the tiger prawn pieces and toss for another 10 seconds in the wok until the prawns start to turn pink. Season with the Shaohsing rice wine and dark soy sauce and cook until the alcohol has evaporated.

Add the cooked jasmine rice and ,using a wooden spoon or metal spatula, start to gently break apart the rice grains: not in a stabbing motion but by tossing the ingredients well for 1–2 minutes.

Drizzle the light soy sauce over the rice and quickly toss to coat the grains well and evenly colour the rice.

Sprinkle over the remaining green parts of the spring onions. Season with a dash of toasted sesame oil and a pinch of ground white pepper and serve immediately with dried chilli flakes on the side.

 Vegan Option Add small cubes of fried tofu instead of the prawns

10 mins 5 mins

Honey Soy Chicken x Mangetout x Walnuts

Serves 1

1 tbsp rapeseed oil

1 garlic clove, finely chopped

100g (3½oz) mini strips of chicken

1 tbsp Shaohsing rice wine or dry sherry

1 tsp dark soy sauce

pinch of Chinese five spice powder

1 small handful of mangetout, sliced into strips

1 small carrot, trimmed and sliced into strips

1 tbsp low-sodium light soy sauce

1 tbsp honey

2–3 roasted walnuts, sliced

cooked jasmine rice (see page 22), to serve

Honey soy chicken with walnuts is a popular Chinese takeaway combination. It has umami, is crunchy and tastes super delicious when wok-fried with sweet mangetout. The Chinese five spice gives a delicate warming hint of spice; it's moreish without overpowering the dish and gives it that *je ne sais quoi*.

Heat a wok over a high heat. Add the rapeseed oil and give it a swirl. Add the garlic, stir-fry for a few seconds, then add the chicken strips and stir-fry for 5 seconds. Season with the Shaohsing rice wine or sherry and dark soy sauce, then add a pinch of Chinese five spice powder and toss for 10 seconds.

Add the mangetout and carrot and toss for a few seconds. Add the light soy sauce and honey and toss everything for 30 seconds until well combined and the chicken is completely cooked through.

Add the sliced walnuts. Serve immediately with jasmine rice.

 Vegan Option Use strips of oyster mushrooms instead of the chicken

15 mins 5 mins

Sweet Soy Chicken x Bamboo Shoot, Sweetcorn & Peanut Fried Rice

Serves 2

1 tbsp rapeseed oil

2.5cm (1in) piece of fresh root ginger, peeled and very finely chopped

1 red chilli, deseeded and finely chopped

1 red onion, finely diced

3 mini chicken fillets, finely diced

pinch of Chinese five spice powder

1 tbsp Shaohsing rice wine

1 tsp dark soy sauce

1 tsp golden syrup

½ × 225g (8oz) can bamboo shoots, drained and diced

160g (5¾oz) can sweetcorn, drained

300g (10½oz) cooked jasmine rice (see page 22)

1–2 tbsp low-sodium light soy sauce

dash of toasted sesame oil

pinch of ground white pepper

To garnish

1 spring onion, trimmed and finely sliced

1 handful of roasted, unsalted peanuts

This is a variation of my grandmother's fried rice. The warming five-spice sweet-soy mixture marries perfectly with tender chicken pieces and earthy, sweet bamboo shoots, and it's topped off with sweetcorn kernels and crunchy peanuts. Yum.

Heat a wok over a medium heat until smoking. Add the rapeseed oil and give it a swirl. Add the ginger, red chilli and red onion and toss for a few seconds, then stir-fry for 20 seconds.

Add the chicken pieces, then the Chinese five spice powder and toss for 1–2 minutes.

Season with the Shaohsing rice wine, dark soy sauce and golden syrup, then toss together well until the chicken pieces are opaque, tender and cooked through.

Add the bamboo shoot pieces, sweetcorn kernels and cooked jasmine rice and, using a wooden spoon or metal spatula, start to gently break apart the rice grains: not in a stabbing motion but by gently tossing and folding for 1–2 minutes.

Add the light soy sauce and toss well to combine. Season with the toasted sesame oil and ground white pepper. Serve immediately, garnished with the spring onion and roasted, unsalted peanuts.

5 mins   5 mins

Cantonese-Style Ham & Egg Fried Rice/Basic Egg Fried Rice

Serves 1–2

2 tbsp rapeseed oil

3 eggs, beaten

70g (2½oz) frozen peas

300g (10½oz) cooked jasmine rice (see page 22)

100g (3½oz) Sticky Char Siu Roast Pork (see page 141), diced to 0.5cm (¼in) cubes

1 tsp dark soy sauce

1–2 tbsp low-sodium light soy sauce

1 tbsp toasted sesame oil

pinch of ground white pepper

1 spring onion, trimmed and finely sliced into rounds, to garnish

chilli oil, to serve

I first tried this dish in a Hong Kong café where it had Chinese ham, peas and pieces of scrambled egg. It was super delicious washed down with a cup of yin yong Cantonese milk tea. And whenever I have this dish, it takes me back to Hong Kong. I'm using cubes of the Sticky Char Siu Roast Pork from page 145, but you can use bacon if you wish – just cook it until it's crispy before you make the rest of the dish. To turn this into basic egg fried rice, just leave out the char siu pork.

Heat a wok over a high heat and add 1 tablespoon of the rapeseed oil. Tip the beaten eggs into the wok and stir to scramble for 3 minutes. Remove and set aside.

Return the wok to the heat and add the remaining tablespoon of rapeseed oil. Heat for 20 seconds, then add the frozen peas and stir-fry for less than a minute. Add the rice and mix well until the rice has broken down. Add the char siu pork pieces and toss together for 1 minute.

Add the scrambled egg pieces back into the wok and stir through. Season with the dark soy sauce, light soy sauce, toasted sesame oil and ground white pepper. Garnish with the spring onion and serve immediately with some chilli oil on the side.

5 mins 5 mins

Bacon x French Beans x Peanuts

Serves 1

1 tbsp rapeseed oil

1 garlic clove, crushed and roughly chopped

1 unsmoked bacon rasher, diced into 1cm (½in) pieces

1 tsp Shaohsing rice wine or dry sherry

1 large handful of French beans, trimmed and sliced into 1cm (½in) rounds

1 tbsp low-sodium light soy sauce

dash or 1 tsp clear rice vinegar

pinch of dried chilli flakes

1 tsp toasted sesame oil

6–8 dry-roasted, unsalted peanuts

cooked rice, to serve

This is a super savoury dish with bags of flavour! The French beans add a sweet, tender bite and the peanuts deliver a moreish crunch. Easy, straightforward and delicious with rice, it won't break the bank.

Heat a wok over a high heat until smoking. Add the rapeseed oil and give it a swirl. Add the garlic and bacon rasher pieces, then toss for a few seconds. Add the Shaohsing rice wine or dry sherry and stir to combine.

Add the French beans and stir-fry for 1 minute until tender.

Season with the light soy sauce, rice vinegar, dried chilli flakes and toasted sesame oil, then add the peanuts.

Serve with a bowl of rice of your choice.

10 mins   5 mins

Soy Minced Pork x Carrot x Courgette

Serves 1

1 tbsp rapeseed oil

1 garlic clove, crushed and roughly chopped

1cm (½in) piece of fresh root ginger, peeled and finely grated

½ red chilli, deseeded and finely chopped

100g (3½oz) minced pork

1 tsp dark soy sauce

1 tsp Shaohsing rice wine

1 carrot, trimmed and sliced into julienne strips on the diagonal

1 courgette, trimmed, halved widthways, then lengthways, then cut into 1cm (½in) strips on the sharp diagonal

1 tbsp low-sodium light soy sauce

pinch of black pepper

dash of toasted sesame oil

cooked rice, to serve

This is an easy dish to throw together: simple and quick. Relying on the classic trio of garlic, ginger and chillies with the store-cupboard umami essentials of light and dark soy, it delivers maximum flavour with minimal fuss. If you don't have minced pork, you could use minced beef or chicken instead.

Heat a wok over a high heat until smoking. Add the rapeseed oil and give it a swirl. Add the garlic, ginger, chilli and minced pork. Toss to stir-fry for a few seconds, then add the dark soy sauce and Shaohsing rice wine to season the mince.

Add the carrot and courgette and stir-fry for 2–3 minutes.

Season with the light soy sauce, pepper and sesame oil. Serve with rice of your choice.

Vegan Option   Swap the minced pork for dehydrated minced soy or tofu minced up in a food processor

Sichuan Pork x Cucumber x Chilli Sauce

Serves 1

1 tbsp rapeseed oil

1 garlic clove, finely chopped

1 red chilli, deseeded
and finely chopped

50g (1¾oz) lean smoked bacon
lardons, finely diced

1 tsp Shaohsing rice wine

⅓ large cucumber, deseeded
and sliced into 0.5cm (¼in)
half-moons

¼ tsp chilli bean sauce

1 tbsp low-sodium light soy sauce

1 tsp golden syrup

1 tsp clear rice vinegar

6–8 roasted, unsalted peanuts

2 sprigs of fresh coriander,
finely chopped

very small pinch of dried chilli flakes

cooked jasmine rice (see page 22),
to serve

Slivers of smoked bacon lardons are tossed with cucumber for a super umami-charged meal. You can use celery slices instead of cucumber to add a fresh, satisfying crunch. This punchy, spicy, tangy, sweet dish is perfect against the backdrop of plain jasmine rice. Once of my favourite combinations ever.

Heat a wok over a high heat. Add the rapeseed oil and give it a swirl. Add the garlic and red chilli, stirring for 3–4 seconds. Add the smoked bacon lardons and stir-fry for 5–10 seconds until caramelized at the edges.

Season with the Shaohsing rice wine. Add the cucumber slices, chilli bean sauce, light soy sauce, golden syrup and clear rice vinegar, and toss well for 10 seconds until the cucumber has softened but still has a slight tender bite.

Add the roasted peanuts. Transfer to a serving plate, sprinkle over the coriander and dried chilli flakes and serve with jasmine rice.

 Vegan Option   Use cubes of smoked tofu, chestnut mushrooms or tempeh pieces instead of the bacon lardons

Wok For Less

10 mins   5 mins

Five Spice Lardons x Red Cabbage Fried Rice

Serves 1

1 tbsp rapeseed oil

1 white onion, finely diced

100g (3½oz) unsmoked lardons, diced

1 tbsp Shaohsing rice wine

½ tsp dark soy sauce

1 large handful red cabbage, shredded

200g (7oz) cooked jasmine rice (see page 22)

1–2 tbsp low-sodium light soy sauce

juice of ½ lemon

dash of toasted sesame oil

pinch of black pepper

1 spring onion, wtrimmed and, finely sliced, to garnish

The savoury, smoky flavours of the bacon contrasted with the sweet, crunchy pepper and bite of the red cabbage in this dish feels totally yin and yang. I love how the acidity of fresh lemon juice makes the dish lighter, which is great for the warmer months. Simple yet delicious with minimal prep time.

Heat a wok over a medium heat until smoking. Add the rapeseed oil and give it a swirl. Add the onion and toss for less than 1 minute. Add the lardon pieces and add the Shaohsing rice wine and toss, again for less than 1 minute.

Season with the dark soy sauce and toss well to coat. Add the red cabbage and toss for 15 seconds until slightly wilted.

Add the jasmine rice and, using a wooden spoon or metal spatula, start to gently break apart the rice grains: not in a stabbing motion but by tossing the ingredients well for 1–2 minutes.

Drizzle over the light soy sauce and then quickly toss to coat the grains well and colour them evenly. Season with the lemon juice, toasted sesame oil and black pepper, garnish with spring onion and serve immediately.

 Vegan Option Use smoked tofu pieces instead of the lardons

5 mins   5 mins

Ham x Peas x Spring Onion

Serves 1

1 tbsp rapeseed oil

1 garlic clove, chopped

2 spring onions, trimmed and sliced into 1cm (½in) rounds, greens and whites separated

150g (5½oz) frozen peas

90g (3oz) honey roast ham, cubed

1 tsp Shaohsing rice wine or dry sherry

1–2 tbsp low-sodium light soy sauce

pinch of ground white pepper

cooked jasmine rice (see page 22), to serve

I love this combo of ham, peas and spring onion – it's perfect in this super quick stir-fry and delicious served with plain jasmine rice. SO good. You can use frozen peas straight from the freezer. You can turn this dish into fried rice by adding cooked leftover jasmine rice after the Shaohsing rice wine. Simple, honest food – love it.

Heat a wok over a high heat until smoking. Add the rapeseed oil and give it a swirl. Add the garlic and whites of the spring onions and toss for a few seconds.

Add the frozen peas and toss for less than 1 minute until all the liquid has evaporated.

Add the ham pieces and the Shaohsing rice wine or dry sherry. Season with the light soy sauce and ground white pepper.

Serve with a bowl of plain jasmine rice and sprinkle over the greens of the spring onions before serving.

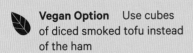

Vegan Option Use cubes of diced smoked tofu instead of the ham

10 mins   6–7 mins

'Everything' Chop Suey

Serves 1

1 tbsp rapeseed oil

1 garlic clove, crushed
and finely chopped

1 red chilli, deseeded
and finely chopped

¼ red onion, sliced

100g (3½oz) mini chicken fillets,
sliced into strips

1 tbsp Shaohsing rice wine
or dry sherry

2–3 raw or cooked tiger prawns,
shelled and deveined and sliced
in half down the middle

30g (1oz) bacon lardons, finely diced

1 tsp dark soy sauce

6 canned water chestnuts or
10 canned bamboo shoots, drained

1 small handful of beansprouts

1 tbsp oyster sauce

¼ tsp chilli bean sauce

1 tbsp low-sodium light soy sauce

2 spring onions, trimmed
and sliced on the diagonal

cooked rice, to serve

This is the epitome of chop suey – everything that you need for a refrigerator clear out! The combination of chicken, prawns and bacon make this a moreish delight, and you could throw in cooked egg noodles at the end, before seasoning with oyster sauce, for the ultimate finale. Add whatever fresh ingredients you have and it will be a winner.

Heat a wok over a high heat until smoking. Add the rapeseed oil and give it a swirl. Add the garlic, chilli and red onion and stir-fry for 5 seconds. Add the chicken strips and let them settle for 5 seconds, then cook, stirring, for 10 seconds.

Add the Shaohsing rice wine and then add the prawns and bacon. Toss for a further 5 seconds. Season with the dark soy sauce and stir to coat all the ingredients.

Add the water chestnuts or bamboo shoots and beansprouts. Season with oyster sauce, chilli bean sauce and light soy sauce. Toss and mix well until well combined and the chicken is completely cooked through.

Sprinkle over the spring onions. Serve with rice of your choice.

Vegan Option   Use smoked tofu instead of the chicken, prawns and bacon, and add sliced shiitake mushrooms

5 mins   5 mins

Oyster Sauce Beef
x Red Onion x Beansprouts

Serves 1

1 tbsp rapeseed oil

2 garlic cloves, finely chopped

1 large red onion, thinly sliced into crescent moons

120g (4¼oz) beef sirloin, sliced into thin beansprout-like strips

1 tbsp Shaohsing rice wine or dry sherry

1 tsp dark soy sauce

1 tbsp oyster sauce

1 handful of beansprouts

1 tbsp low-sodium light soy sauce

1 spring onion, trimmed and sliced into 1cm (½in) rounds, to garnish

cooked jasmine rice (see page 22), to serve

This is a delicious supper that won't cost the earth, making the beef the star of the show with a little going a long way. The oyster sauce delivers maximum umami and the beansprouts add a tender crunch. This is a perfect match with some jasmine rice.

Heat a wok over a high heat until smoking. Add the rapeseed oil and give it a swirl. Add the garlic and toss for a couple of seconds, then add the red onion, toss for 5 seconds, and then add the beef. Let it settle for a couple of seconds, then add the Shaohsing rice wine or sherry and toss well. Add the dark soy sauce and oyster sauce and toss again. Follow with the beansprouts and toss for 1 minute until they are tender.

Season with the light soy sauce and garnish with the spring onion. Serve immediately with jasmine rice.

Vegan Option   Use sliced mushrooms or strips of smoked tofu instead of the beef

2.

Eggs-citing on a Budget

2   Eggs-citing on a Budget

I've always been impressed by the Asian clever use of eggs in classic, simple and honest straightforward recipes. Eggs are an egg-cellent source of quality protein and full of nutritious iron, vitamins, carotenoids and other minerals. Always try to buy free-range eggs where you can for better health for both the animals and you.

You don't need to be eating two eggs a day, but you could have them perhaps once a week as part of a balanced diet. I feel strongly that if we cut spending on processed, sugary, nutrient-lacking foods and invest the money wisely on healthy, inexpensive ingredients such as eggs, we can take a step toward healthier and budget-boosting goals.

As with all my recipes in this book, a little goes a long way. If you don't eat eggs, then this chapter may not be for you, but I have given vegan substitute options for many of the recipes, so I hope you still give them a go. All the recipes serve one or two, can be easily doubled up for family occasions and work well with other dishes.

5 mins   5 mins

Soy Egg & Broccoli Scramble

Serves 1

1 tbsp rapeseed oil

pinch of salt

1 broccoli stalk, peeled
and sliced into strips

2 eggs, lightly beaten

1 spring onion, trimmed and finely
diced or ½ red chilli, deseeded
and finely diced

To serve

1 tsp of low-sodium light soy
sauce or your favourite hot sauce

toast or cooked jasmine rice
(see page 22)

This is the perfect dish for a light lunch or supper. I usually keep broccoli stalks. Here you just peel off the tough outer edges, slice the inner stalks, stir-fry them until tender and then scramble them with some eggs, diced spring onions or red chilli. Serve either on its own or with rice or a piece of toast, with a dash of light soy sauce over the top.

Heat a wok over a medium heat until slightly smoking. Add the rapeseed oil. Sprinkle in the pinch of salt, stir for just a second, then add the broccoli stalk strips. Toss and stir for 1–2 minutes until tender.

Pour in the beaten eggs and toss to scramble the eggs until fluffy or cooked to your liking. This should take less than 30 seconds. Sprinkle over the spring onion. Transfer to a plate on top of toast or jasmine rice. Drizzle over the light soy sauce or your favourite hot sauce. Enjoy.

 Vegan Option   Use smoked
tofu blitzed in a food processor
and seasoned with turmeric
instead of the eggs

5 mins 5 mins

Egg & Tomato Spring Onion Scramble

Serves 1

1 tbsp rapeseed oil

pinch of salt

1 ripe beef tomato, sliced into strips

2 eggs, lightly beaten

1 spring onion, trimmed and sliced into 1cm (½in) rounds

To serve

toast or cooked jasmine rice (see page 22)

1 tsp low-sodium light soy sauce

This is a simple egg, tomato and spring onion scramble. In China, this classic dish is called 'xi hong si' which means 'tomatoes' but is transliterated as 'Western red', which is basically derived from 'that Western, red-looking vegetable'... And this is now a home-style family favourite. The tomatoes have umami, the spring onions add a fresh bite and the eggs are fluffy and rich. Delicious on its own or served on top of a slice of toast or with rice.

Heat a wok over a medium heat until slightly smoking. Add the rapeseed oil. Sprinkle in the salt, stir for just a second, then add the tomato pieces. Toss and stir for a few seconds.

Pour in the beaten eggs and toss to scramble the eggs until fluffy or cooked to your liking; this should take less than 30 seconds.

Sprinkle over the spring onion. Transfer to a plate, on top of a slice of toast or over jasmine rice, then drizzle over a dash of light soy sauce. Enjoy.

Vegan Option Use smoked tofu blitzed in a food processor and seasoned with turmeric instead of the eggs

5 mins   5 mins

Fold Over Chinese-Style Stuffed Egg Omelette

Serves 1

2 eggs, lightly beaten

1 tsp low-sodium light soy sauce

dash of toasted sesame oil

1 spring onion, trimmed and finely chopped

pinch of ground white pepper

1 tbsp rapeseed oil

hot sauce or sweet chilli sauce, to serve

For the filling

a few strips of cooked ham, smoked salmon, or cooked chicken breast pieces

1 small handful of shredded iceberg or Gem lettuce

I love this kind of omelette. This style of cooking an omelette is not necessarily Asian but more Western, though stuffing one with your favourite ingredients is rather an Asian way of eating! Growing up, my mother would make this kind of East-meets-West omelette; sometimes the filling would include pickled carrots and cucumber and it might be topped with pork floss. Use whatever you have in the refrigerator; smoked salmon, shredded smoked ham, strips of chicken breast or pickled vegetables would work well.

In a small bowl, mix the beaten eggs with the light soy sauce, toasted sesame oil, spring onion and ground white pepper.

Heat a wok or pan over a medium heat until slightly smoking. Add the rapeseed oil and give it a swirl. Add the seasoned egg mix, tilting the wok or pan to coat the sides: you want a circular golden base. Cook for 40 seconds over a low–medium heat.

Using a flat wooden spoon, gently lift the egg base away from the pan, then flip it (like a pancake). Cook on the other side for 10 seconds until firm.

Transfer to a serving plate. In the centre add the strips of ham, smoked salmon or chicken breast, then fold the omelette in half over the filling. Top with shredded lettuce. Serve warm with your favourite hot sauce or sweet chilli sauce.

15 mins

6–8 mins

Scotch Egg Miso Mushroom Ramen

Serves 2

For the broth

1 tbsp rapeseed oil

2.5cm (1in) piece of fresh root ginger, peeled and finely grated

1 tbsp red miso paste

500ml (18fl oz) just-boiled water

100ml (3½fl oz) oat milk

1 large handful of mushrooms (any mushroom will do)

For the noodles

200g (7oz) ramen noodles

1 tsp toasted sesame oil

2 tsp low-sodium light soy sauce

To serve

1 Scotch egg, sliced in half

1 tbsp canned sweetcorn, drained

½ piece of nori seaweed, sliced into rectangles

½ red chilli, deseeded and sliced into thin julienne strips

1 spring onion, trimmed and finely sliced

I love a mushroom ramen with a moreish umami broth that comes from the combination of good-quality miso paste and oat milk. You can buy dry or frozen ramen noodles that you can defrost for a super speedy dinner or just use fresh egg noodles. Serving this ramen with half a porky Scotch egg on the side is one of my guilty pleasures. Or you could just serve it with some halved boiled eggs. Enjoy!

Heat a wok to a medium heat until lightly smoking. Add the rapeseed oil and give it a swirl. Add the ginger, stir for just a second, then add the miso paste and the measured hot water. Using a whisk, mix the miso and water well. Bring to a simmer.

Stir in the oat milk, then add the mushrooms. Reduce the heat to low while you cook the noodles.

Bring a small pan of water to the boil, then cook the ramen noodles according to the packet instructions. Drain, run under cold water, drain again and then drizzle over the toasted sesame oil to prevent them from sticking together.

Place 1 teaspoon of the light soy sauce at the bottom of each serving bowl. Divide the noodles between the 2 bowls. Pour the hot broth over the noodles, reserving the mushrooms. Arrange the mushrooms on top of the noodles. Place half a Scotch egg on each, top with the sweetcorn, nori and chilli, then sprinkle over the spring onion. Serve immediately.

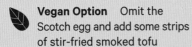

Vegan Option Omit the Scotch egg and add some strips of stir-fried smoked tofu

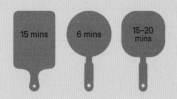

15 mins   6 mins   15–20 mins

Taiwanese Cold Egg Noodle Salad 'Liang Mein'

Serves 2

For the egg omelette strips

1 tbsp rapeseed oil

2 eggs, beaten

For the noodles

300g (10½oz) dried ramen noodles

toasted sesame oil

For the dressing

2 garlic cloves, minced

2 tbsp tahini

3 tbsp low-sodium light soy sauce

2 tbsp mirin

1 tbsp toasted sesame oil

2 tbsp clear rice vinegar

1 tsp chilli bean sauce

To serve

¼ cucumber, sliced into strips

1 small carrot, trimmed and sliced into julienne strips

pinch of dried chilli flakes or Japanese shichimi togarashi chilli flakes

I love a refreshing cold liang mein noodle on a hot summer's day. This classic Taiwanese dish is quite versatile and you could use cooked tiger prawns or strips of chicken breast instead of the omelette, or beansprouts if you are vegan; but I think the combination of eggy omelette strips with a rich sesame dressing against crunchy carrots and cucumber makes this combo the most delicious. Choose your noodles wisely – the best are shanghai noodles (thin, rounded wheat-flour noodles) or ramen noodles, for overall texture and crunch. Enjoy!

Heat a wok or pan over a medium heat until slightly smoking. Add the rapeseed oil and give it a swirl. Add the egg mix, tilting the wok or pan to coat the sides: you want a circular golden base. Cook for 40 seconds over a low–medium heat.

Using a flat wooden spoon, gently lift the base away from the pan, then flip it (like a pancake). Cook on the other side for 10 seconds until firm. Transfer to a chopping board and slice into strips. Set aside to cool.

Bring a small pan of water to the boil, then cook the ramen noodles according to the packet instructions. Drain, run under cold water, drain again and then drizzle over a little toasted sesame oil to prevent them from sticking together. Chill in the refrigerator for 15–20 minutes with the cucumber and carrots.

In a small bowl, mix together the dressing ingredients and then set aside.

To serve, transfer the noodles to serving bowls. Top with the cucumber, carrots and egg omelette strips. Sprinkle over the dried chilli flakes and serve with the dressing on the side. To eat, toss everything together well and eat immediately.

15 mins   10 mins

Taiwanese Lun Piah or Run Bing Pancake

Makes 8 pancakes • Serves 4

For the crunchy vegetables

1 carrot, trimmed and cut into julienne strips

⅓ cucumber, deseeded and cut into julienne strips

80g (2¾oz) beansprouts, blanched

For the peanut sugar sprinkle

60g (2¼oz) roasted, salted peanuts

2 tbsp golden caster sugar

For the egg omelette

3 eggs, lightly beaten

2 tbsp rapeseed oil

For the 'pancake'

150g (5½oz) bread flour

225ml (8fl oz) cold water

1 tbsp coconut oil, melted

pinch of sea salt

pinch of sugar

To serve

½ tsp chilli bean sauce (optional)

½ tsp hoisin sauce

julienne strips of tofu

a few sprigs of fresh coriander

This savoury, filled street-food pancake is perfectly light for summer. You could fill it with whatever you like but I love slices of egg omelette with humble crunchy carrot, cucumber and beansprouts. It's the peanut sugar sprinkles that make this one super moreish. Use a non-stick pancake pan on the lowest heat possible for the best results. This dish can also be served at important family gatherings or Chinese festivals as the 'spring roll' shape can represent 'wealth' or 'bars of gold'.

Prepare all the crunchy vegetable ingredients, and chill, covered, in the refrigerator until ready to use.

To make the peanut sugar sprinkle, place the roasted, salted peanuts in a mini food processor, then pulse until they have a coarse texture. Add the golden caster sugar, mix well and spoon out on a small dish ready for sprinkling. Set aside.

Make the egg omelette by heating a small pan over a medium heat. Add the rapeseed oil and give it a swirl. Pour in the beaten egg mixture, tilting the pan to coat the bottom. Cook for 40 seconds until golden. Using a flat rubber spatula, gently loosen the cooked omelette from the base of the pan and transfer to a chopping board. Slice into 0.5 × 5cm (¼ × 2in) strips. Set aside.

In a bowl, gently mix the flour, measured cold water, melted coconut oil, salt and sugar into a batter. Heat a non-stick crêpe pan over a low–medium heat. Dip a pastry brush into the batter and then paint the batter straight on the pan in a circular motion, until the base of the pan is coated! (Work quickly, brushing a thin layer all over.) When the base of the pancake is golden and easily loosens from the pan, use a rubber spatula to lift the pancake out of the pan. Place on a plate and cover to keep warm. Repeat until you have made about 8 pancakes.

Eat these pancakes at room temperature, perfect for the summer weather. To assemble, spoon some hoisin sauce and chilli bean sauce (if you like it spicy) on the base, top with some carrot, cucumber, beansprouts, egg omelette strips, tofu strips and coriander. Sprinkle over the peanut sugar, roll and eat immediately.

20 mins

20–25 mins

Macanese Minchi Hash

Serves 2 to share

For the rice

350g (12oz) jasmine rice

300ml (10fl oz) water

For the potatoes

500g (1lb 2oz) baby potatoes, unpeeled and cut into 1cm (½in) dice

olive oil, for drizzling

pinch of salt

pinch of ground black pepper

1–2 pinches dried chilli flakes

For the pork

1 tbsp rapeseed oil

1 large white onion, diced

2 bay leaves

1 garlic clove, finely chopped

200g (7oz) lean minced pork

1 tbsp Shaohsing rice wine

1–2 tbsp oyster sauce

1–2 tbsp low-sodium light soy sauce

1–2 tbsp Worcestershire sauce

1 tsp dark soy sauce, or more to taste

pinch of ground white pepper

For the fried eggs

1 tbsp rapeseed oil

2 eggs

pinch of salt

pinch of ground white pepper

2 large spring onions, trimmed and sliced into 1cm (½in) rounds, to garnish

 Vegan Option Use rehydrated minced soy instead of minced pork, and mushroom sauce instead of oyster sauce

This is one comforting brunch dish! This dish is traditionally wok-fried pork with some soy sauce and fried potatoes served with runny fried eggs on top and is utterly delicious when accompanied by jasmine rice. It's so good that you'll want to have it all the time!

Preheat the oven to 180°C (350°F), Gas Mark 4.

Wash the rice well until the water runs clear (see page 22). Place in a medium saucepan and cover with the measured water. Bring to the boil, uncovered, then reduce the heat to low, cover with the lid and cook for 15–20 minutes until the rice is fluffy.

Meanwhile, place the potato cubes on a roasting tray, drizzle over olive oil and season with salt, ground black pepper and dried chilli flakes. Place in the oven and roast for 15–20 minutes.

Set aside the rice and roast potatoes and keep warm.

To cook the pork, heat a wok over a high heat until smoking. Add the rapeseed oil and give it a swirl. Add the onion and fry for 2 minutes until translucent.

Add the bay leaves and garlic, followed by the minced pork. Let it settle for 45 seconds to sear and brown on one side, then begin to flip and toss to cook it on the other side, about 3–4 minutes.

Before the pork is completely cooked, add the Shaohsing rice wine. Season with the oyster sauce, light soy sauce, Worcestershire sauce, dark soy sauce and ground white pepper. Toss well until the seasoning has coated the minced pork.

Add the roasted potato pieces to the wok and toss together for 1 minute. Season further to taste. Remove from the heat.

Fire up a frying pan over a medium heat for the eggs. Add the rapeseed oil, then crack in each egg and fry for 1 minute, or until the bottom is crispy but the egg yolks are still runny on the top. Season with the salt and ground white pepper.

On a large serving plate, place the rice in the centre, pour the minced pork and potato (minchi) over the top, then lay the fried eggs on top of the minchi. Garnish with a final sprinkle of spring onions. Serve immediately.

10 mins   15 mins

Chicken & Sweetcorn Egg-Drop Wonton Skin Soup

Serves 2

1 tbsp rapeseed oil

2.5cm (1in) piece of fresh root ginger, peeled and finely grated

4 mini chicken fillets, finely diced

1 tsp Shaohsing rice wine

1 litre (1¾ pints) vegetable stock

325g (11½oz) can sweetcorn, drained

1 tsp vegetable bouillon powder

1 tbsp low-sodium light soy sauce

dash of toasted sesame oil

pinch of ground white pepper

3 tbsp cornflour

2 tbsp cold water

1 egg, lightly beaten

3–4 pieces of wonton skins, fresh or frozen and defrosted, either sliced in half on the diagonal or each cut into 5 equal strips

2 spring onions, trimmed and finely sliced

This is a delicious and moreish soup. I love chicken sweetcorn soup and a good soup like this cannot be complete without the 'egg flower drop' pattern that comes with adding a beaten egg at the end, to create the creamy texture and classic and distinctive swirling pattern. To make this dish a substantial meal, I add some sliced pieces of fresh wonton skins, which I usually have to hand in my freezer. Just defrost them, slice them into strips and they become chunky noodle strips once parboiled in the soup. Great as a light supper. Enjoy!

Heat a wok over a medium heat until lightly smoking. Add the rapeseed oil and give it a swirl. Add the ginger, stir for just a second, then add the chicken pieces and stir-fry for 1 minute.

Add the Shaohsing rice wine, pour in the vegetable stock and bring to a simmer.

Add the canned sweetcorn. Season the soup with the bouillon powder, light soy sauce, sesame oil and ground white pepper. Bring to the boil.

In a small bowl, combine the cornflour and measured cold water to make a slurry. Stir into the soup to thicken.

Using a spoon, stir the soup in a circular motion and gently pour in the beaten egg. This will help you make the swirling web-like pattern with the egg. Add the wonton pieces and cook for less than 1 minute until softened.

Transfer to 2 bowls, top with the spring onions and serve immediately.

10 mins
+
10 mins
marinating

4–5 mins

Chinese-Style Oyster Sauce Beef Egg Omelette

Serves 2

For the beef

120g (4¼oz) tender beef rump fillet, diced

¼ tsp bicarbonate of soda

2.5cm (1in) piece of fresh root ginger, peeled and finely grated

2 tsp oyster sauce

1 tbsp low-sodium light soy sauce

2 pinches of ground white pepper

1 tbsp cornflour

1 tsp dark soy sauce

1 tbsp rapeseed oil

For the eggs

2 eggs

pinch of salt

1 tsp cornflour

pinch of ground white pepper

10g (¼oz) spring onions, trimmed and sliced

1 tbsp rapeseed oil

cooked jasmine rice (see page 22) or salad leaves (optional), to serve

1 tsp chilli oil

This makes a super delicious quick supper and the perfect dish to exemplify the Chinese tradition of 'a little goes a long way'. The small rump pieces of beef are used to flavour the eggy omelette, giving a beefy umami flavour. Slice it like pizza and serve with jasmine rice. Kids will love this as a quick – and nutritious – after-school dinner. You can also use diced ham, prawns or mushrooms instead of the beef.

Place the beef pieces in a bowl, add the bicarbonate of soda, ginger, oyster sauce, light soy sauce, ground white pepper and cornflour. Let it marinate for 10 minutes.

In another bowl, lightly beat the eggs, then add the salt, cornflour and ground white pepper along with some of the spring onions. Lightly stir to mix together and set aside.

Heat a wok over a medium heat until lightly smoking. Add the rapeseed oil and give it a swirl. Add the marinated beef. Let it settle for 15 seconds and then stir-fry for 1 minute until tender and cooked through.

Add the dark soy sauce and the remaining rapeseed oil. Pour in the beaten egg mixture and let it settle for 30 seconds. Reduce the heat and cook for 2½–3 minutes until the egg omelette is fluffy.

Using a flat rubber spatula or a wooden spoon, loosen the base of the omelette and transfer to a serving plate. You can slice it into 4 pieces like a pizza for sharing, if you like. Drizzle over your favourite chilli oil, top with the rest of the spring onions and serve with jasmine rice or salad leaves, or on its own.

15 mins   20 mins

Cantonese-Style Macaroni Soup

Serves 2 or 4 to share

3 ripe tomatoes, sliced

800ml (1½ pints) boiling water

1 tbsp vegetable bouillon powder

200g (7oz) canned plum tomatoes, along with their juices

3 eggs, lightly beaten

1 tbsp low-sodium light soy sauce

dash of toasted sesame oil

pinch of salt

pinch of ground white pepper

1 tsp chilli bean sauce or sriracha chilli sauce, or to taste

300g (10½oz) cooked macaroni pasta, dressed in a little olive or rapeseed oil

200g (7oz) can sweetcorn

1 tbsp cornflour, blended with 2 tbsp cold water

1 head of pak choy, shredded or 1 large handful of baby spinach (optional)

2 spring onions, trimmed and finely sliced

A classic dish served in many of the licensed street vendors (dai pai dongs) offering Hong Kongers a quick snack. Add a little chilli bean sauce or sriracha for a slightly spicy kick. This is pure comfort in a bowl; inexpensive homely food at its best. I use canned plum tomatoes for a rich, tart flavour.

If you want to skin the fresh tomatoes before chopping, bring a wok or pan of water to the boil. Cut a small cross at the base of each tomato and plunge them into the boiling water for less than 1 minute, then drain. The skin will peel off easily. Finely chop the flesh, discarding the hard centre.

Pour the boiling water into a wok. Stir in the bouillon powder and bring to a simmer, then add the fresh tomatoes and cook over a medium heat for 5 minutes until the tomatoes have softened.

Add the canned plum tomatoes with their juices and bring to a simmer.

Pour the beaten eggs into the broth, gently stirring. Add the light soy sauce, sesame oil, salt, white pepper, chilli or sriracha sauce, cooked macaroni, sweetcorn and blended cornflour mixture. Mix well and heat through.

If using, add the pak choy or baby spinach and let it wilt. Garnish with the spring onion and serve immediately.

10 mins   6–8 mins

Spam and Eggy
Chow Mein

Serves 2

1 tbsp rapeseed oil

2 garlic cloves, minced

1 red chilli, deseeded
and finely chopped

100g (3½oz) Spam or honey
roast ham, cubed

½ tbsp dark soy sauce

350g (12oz) cooked egg noodles

1 tbsp low-sodium light soy sauce

2 eggs, lightly beaten

1 tsp toasted sesame oil

1–2 pinches of ground white pepper

2 spring onions, trimmed
and finely sliced

hot sauce, to serve

**This kind of chow mein is simple and comforting and perfect
for an emergency supper. It may not be the healthiest
of dishes, but the combination of Spam and egg is so good and
always hits the spot. It's perfect served with a side of hot
sauce. You could use honey roast ham instead of the Spam.**

Heat a wok over a high heat until smoking. Add the rapeseed
oil and give it a swirl. Add the garlic and chilli and stir-fry for
a few seconds.

Add the Spam or honey roast ham pieces, then add the
dark soy sauce and toss well. Add the cooked egg noodles and
season with light soy sauce, then toss together well.

Make a well in the middle of the pan and pour in the beaten
egg mixture, stirring to scramble to your liking for about 30 seconds.

Season with the toasted sesame oil and ground white pepper
and garnish with the spring onions. Give all the ingredients one
last toss and serve immediately with some hot sauce.

Vegan Option   Use smoked
tofu cubes instead of spam
and wheat-flour noodles
instead of egg noodles

3.

Fast, Fresh, Flavourful Noodles

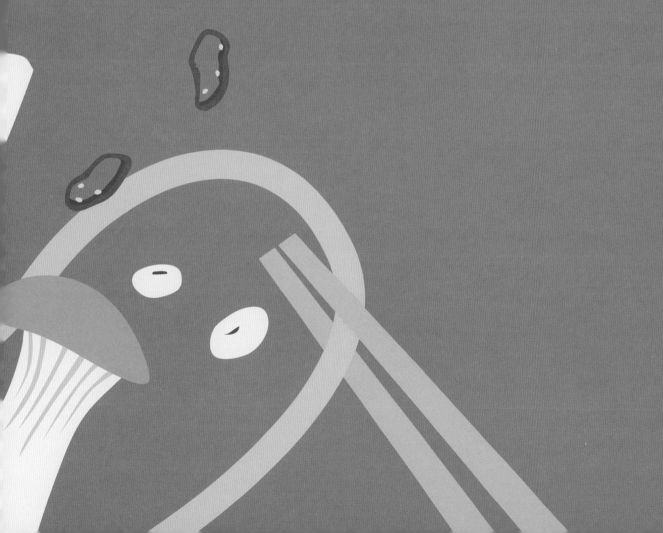

3 Fast, Fresh, Flavourful Noodles

In this chapter, I've included all my staple noodle dishes: mid-week suppers that won't cost the earth and are far cheaper than eating out. Noodles are fast, fresh and inexpensive.

A couple require a bit more effort, like my Malaysian-Style Smoked Mackerel with Egg Laksa Curry (see page 79) or my Shanghainese-Style Mini 'Cloud' Wonton Noodle Soup (see page 66). But I've pared down my Simple Singapore Noodles (see page 86) by using cooked rice noodles and prepared stir-fry veggies, which makes the dish super quick and easy. There's also my Saucy Oyster Sauce Beef & Broccoli Chow Mein (see page 84) and Bang Bang Chicken Peanut Noodles (see page 86) – spicy peanut noodles are a winner. As are the Japanese Teriyaki Beef Udon Noodle Stir-Fry (see page 88), Buddha's Chow Mein (see page 71) and my Malaysian-inspired Hakka Pork Mee (see page 85). I hope you enjoy this chapter; there's certainly something for everyone.

30–40 mins

5 mins

Shanghainese-Style Mini 'Cloud' Wonton Noodle Soup

Serves 2

For the wontons (makes 50–60)

300g (10½oz) minced lean pork

½ tsp salt

1 tsp cornflour

1 tsp Shaohsing rice wine

1 spring onion, trimmed and finely diced

50–60 wheat-flour dumpling wrappers

For the soup

600ml (20fl oz) filtered water

1 tsp vegetable bouillon powder

2.5cm (1in) piece of fresh root ginger, peeled and finely grates (optional)

1 tbsp low-sodium light soy sauce

1 tsp toasted sesame oil

baby pak choy leaves

To serve

200g (7oz) cooked egg noodles, rinsed and refreshed in hot water

2 spring onions, trimmed and finely sliced

Vegan Option
Use vegetarian sausage meat instead of the minced pork and wheat flour noodles instead of egg noodles

I first tried this soup in the Intercontinental Hotel in Shanghai. They had a wok station with a chef making the smallest but freshest, most delicious mini wontons. They were tiny; the meatball size was less than a teaspoon and they had the softest dough that melted in the mouth. They were served in a rich chicken broth with spring onions – just simple and moreish. I love adding egg noodles to this dish. The wontons make a huge batch so you can freeze them and cook from frozen – perfect for an emergency lunch or dinner.

In a bowl, add the minced lean pork and add the salt, cornflour, Shaohsing rice wine and spring onion. Mix well.

Taking about 5g (⅛oz), or less than a teaspoon, of the filling, place it in the centre of a wheat-flour dumpling wrapper and fold tightly around the filling to make a pouch, then bring both sides to the centre, pinching and twisting to secure. Set aside on a lightly floured tray, then repeat with the rest of the filling and dumplings. Set aside 20 wonton dumplings and pack the rest up into plastic containers and place in the freezer. To save space, after they have been in the freezer for half a day, you can transfer them into freezer-proof bags. To cook from frozen, just boil in some soup stock for 6–7 minutes.

Heat a wok or pan over a medium heat and fill with the measured water. Season with the vegetable bouillon powder, add the ginger, light soy sauce and toasted sesame oil and bring to a simmer. Drop in the 20 reserved dumplings and cook for 5 minutes until they float to the surface. Gently move the cooking broth, without over stirring or breaking the dumplings, waiting until the wontons float to the surface. Stir in some baby pak choy leaves to wilt them.

Divide the warm cooked egg noodles between 2 bowls, spoon over the broth and 10 wonton dumplings with some baby pak choy into each. Sprinkle over the spring onions and serve immediately.

10 mins 7 mins

Hoisin Cauliflower Noodles

Serves 2

1 tbsp rapeseed oil

1 small head of cauliflower, washed and broken into florets

50ml (2fl oz) water

For the sauce

1 tbsp rapeseed oil

2.5cm (1in) piece of fresh root ginger, peeled and finely grated

1 red chilli, deseeded and finely chopped

200ml (7fl oz) vegetable bouillon stock (1 tsp vegetable bouillon powder + 200ml/7fl oz cold water)

2 tbsp hoisin sauce

1–2 tbsp low-sodium light soy sauce

1 tsp dark soy sauce

1 tbsp cornflour, blended with 2 tbsp cold water

200g (7oz) cooked egg noodles

To garnish

1 handful of roasted, unsalted peanuts

1 tbsp finely sliced spring onions

I love wok-charring cauliflower to bring out its smoky sweet flavours. It makes the perfect accompaniment to either chunky egg noodles or wide rice noodles. I like umami sauces especially savoury hoisin sauce. The combination of aromatic chives and crunchy peanuts makes this a super satisfying dish. So good.

Heat a wok over a high heat until smoking. Add the rapeseed oil and give it a swirl. Add the cauliflower florets and stir-fry for 30 seconds, then drizzle the measured water around the edges of the wok to create some steam to help cook the florets. Keep stirring until any liquid has evaporated, charring the florets for a smoky flavour. Remove the florets and set aside.

Wash the wok, and reheat for the sauce, adding the rapeseed oil. Add the ginger and red chilli and fry for a few seconds. Then add the vegetable stock, seasoning it with hoisin sauce, light soy sauce and dark soy sauce, and thicken it with the cornflour slurry for a glossy sauce.

Add the cooked egg noodles and the cauliflower back in and toss in the sauce well, garnish with peanuts and finely sliced spring onions and serve immediately.

20 mins 5 mins

Buddha's Chow Mein

Serves 2

1 tbsp rapeseed oil

100g (3½oz) baby leeks, sliced into 2.5cm (1in) pieces on the diagonal

25g (1oz) dried Chinese mushrooms, soaked in warm water for 20 minutes, drained, stalks discarded, and cut into 1cm (½in) slices

½ tsp dark soy sauce

1 tbsp Shaohsing rice wine or dry sherry

300g (10½oz) cooked thin egg noodles, drained and dressed with 1 tsp toasted sesame oil

1 tbsp mushroom sauce

1 tbsp golden syrup

2 tbsp low-sodium light soy sauce

1 handful of beansprouts

1 tsp toasted sesame oil

2 spring onions, trimmed and finely sliced, to garnish

This is a simple yet rich-tasting dish. The trick is to find plump dried Chinese mushrooms, which can be bought from a Chinese supermarket. Their earthy umami, meaty flavour contrasts beautifully with the texture of the egg noodles. A classic Chinese dish that not only hits the budget but is incredibly moreish thanks to the Chinese mushrooms.

Heat a wok over a high heat until smoking. Add the rapeseed oil and give it a swirl. Add the baby leeks and toss for 30 seconds, then add the rehydrated sliced mushrooms and toss for 10 seconds to release their flavours. Add the dark soy sauce and toss well, then add the Shaohsing rice wine or dry sherry and cook until evaporated.

Add the cooked egg noodles and toss together well for 30 seconds, then season with the mushroom sauce, golden syrup and light soy sauce. Add the beansprouts and gently toss and fold into the dish. Season with the toasted sesame oil, then garnish with the spring onions and serve immediately.

10 mins   5 mins

Spicy Mushroom Egg Noodles

Serves 2

1 tbsp rapeseed oil

2 garlic cloves, finely chopped

1 tbsp finely chopped red chilli

200g (7oz) fresh shiitake mushrooms

1 tbsp Shaohsing rice wine

2 tbsp low-sodium light soy sauce

200g (7oz) cooked egg noodles

1 tsp dark soy sauce

1 tsp cornflour

1 tbsp cold water

2 spring onions, trimmed and finely sliced

50g (1¾oz) toasted pine nuts

pinch of dried chilli flakes

1 tbsp chilli oil, for drizzling

This easy wok-fried dish of spicy shiitake mushroom noodles is super simple to make but packs an umami punch. It hits the spot when you're pushed for time.

Heat the wok over a high heat until slightly smoking. Add the rapeseed oil and give it a swirl. Add the garlic and chilli and stir for a few seconds, then add the shiitake mushrooms and toss for 1–2 minutes. Add the Shaohsing rice wine and light soy sauce and toss well.

Add the cooked egg noodles and stir to mix. Season with the dark soy sauce.

In a small bowl, mix the cornflour with the measured cold water to make a cornflour slurry and then pour this into the wok. Mix well.

Toss in the spring onions, pine nuts and chilli flakes. Drizzle with chilli oil and serve immediately.

 Vegan Option Use thin wheat-flour noodles instead of egg noodles

15 mins　　30 mins

Soy Braised Sweet Potato & Chickpea Ramen

Serves 2 or 4 to share

1.2 litres (2 pints) filtered water

2.5cm (1in) piece of fresh root ginger, peeled and sliced into coins and then strips

3 baby shallots, sliced in half

1 red chilli, deseeded and sliced into long strips

2 large tomatoes, quartered

400g (14oz) sweet potato, trimmed, peeled and sliced into 1.5cm (¾in) cubes

400g (14oz) can chickpeas, drained and rinsed

1 stick of cinnamon bark

2 star anise

4–5 tbsp low-sodium light soy sauce

2 tbsp golden syrup

For the noodles

1 litre (1¾ pints) water

200g (7oz) ramen noodles

1 tsp toasted sesame oil

To garnish

50g (1¾oz) Baby Gem lettuce leaves, halved, leaves separated

1 small handful of fresh coriander, chopped

1 tsp chilli oil

Taiwan meets Japan in this dish where sweet potatoes never tasted so good. This comforting sweet, soy-spiced noodle soup is perfect for wintry cold months and it's quick and satisfying to make. Fresh sweet potatoes are braised in light soy sauce, golden syrup, ginger, star anise and cinnamon. Canned chickpeas are super economical; serve on chunky ramen noodles with some wilted iceberg or romaine lettuce and sprinkled with coriander. You could use tofu or mushrooms, if you like, instead of chickpeas and sweet potatoes.

Heat the measured filtered water in a wok until simmering. Add the ginger, shallots, chillies, tomatoes, sweet potatoes, chickpeas, cinnamon bark and star anise, then add the light soy sauce and golden syrup. Simmer, uncovered, for 30 minutes over a medium heat.

Five minutes before the broth is cooked, bring the 1 litre (1¾ pints) of water to a boil. Add the ramen noodles, then boil for 3 minutes until al dente. Drain, then rinse under cold running water. Drizzle over the toasted sesame oil to prevent the noodles from sticking together. Divide them between 2–4 serving bowls and set aside.

Just before serving, add the lettuce leaves to the broth and blanch for 5 seconds.

To serve, pour 3–4 ladles of the broth into each of the serving bowls, then add the sweet potato and chickpeas. Decorate each bowl with the wilted lettuce leaves. Garnish with the fresh coriander, add a drizzle of the chilli oil for a spicy kick, then serve immediately.

10 mins   5 mins

Simple Singapore Noodles

Serves 2–3

For the sauce

2 tbsp low-sodium light soy sauce

1 tsp dark soy sauce

1 tbsp vegetarian mushroom sauce

2 tbsp sweet chilli sauce

1 tbsp rice vinegar

1 tsp toasted sesame oil

For the stir-fry

140g (5oz) vermicelli rice noodles

2 tbsp rapeseed oil

2.5cm (1in) piece of fresh root
ginger, peeled and finely grated

1 red chilli, deseeded
and finely chopped

100g (3½oz) fresh shiitake
mushrooms, stalks removed
(save these for a vegetable
stock), and sliced

½ tsp ground turmeric

200g (7oz) crunchy fried tofu
(see recipe into)

300g (10½oz) bag of mixed
stir-fry vegetables

1 tbsp Shaohsing rice wine
or vegetable stock

½ tsp toasted sesame oil

1 tsp low-sodium light soy sauce

½–1 tsp dried chilli flakes

To serve

1 red chilli, deseeded
and sliced into fine strips

fresh coriander leaves

chilli oil

These are the most simple and delicious Singapore noodles. The trick is to use shop-bought ready-fried crunchy tofu which you can get from Asian supermarkets and a bag of mixed stir-fry vegetables, plus fresh cooked rice noodles. With just a few store-cupboard seasonings, this flavour-packed dinner can be on the table in minutes.

Mix all the sauce ingredients together in a jug.

Place the noodles in just-boiled water and soak them for 3 minutes until the water turns opaque white. Drain and rinse the noodles well. Or use fresh cooked rice noodles.

Heat a wok over a medium–high heat until slightly smoking. Add the rapeseed oil and give it a swirl. Add the ginger and chilli and stir for 1 second. Quickly add the shiitake mushrooms and turmeric and give it another quick stir for a second. Add the shop-bought crunchy tofu and toss well. Add the stir-fry vegetables and stir for 1–2 minutes. Add the Shaohsing rice wine or vegetable stock to deglaze the wok.

Add the soaked rice noodles and then pour in the sauce. Toss for 1 minute until any liquid in the wok has evaporated and the noodles have softened but still have a bite. Season with the toasted sesame oil and light soy sauce and sprinkle over the dried chilli flakes.

Transfer to a serving plate and garnish with the fresh red chillies and coriander. Serve with some chilli oil and eat immediately.

10 mins   5 mins

Spicy Peanut Noodles

Serves 2

For the peanut sauce

3 garlic cloves, minced

1 red chilli, deseeded
and finely chopped

4 tbsp smooth roasted
peanut butter

50ml (2fl oz) warm water

2 tbsp dark soy sauce

2 tbsp seasoned rice vinegar

2 tbsp golden syrup

For the noodles

200g (7oz) dried knife-cut
noodles or flat udon noodles

1 tsp toasted sesame oil

To serve

chopped fresh coriander leaves

1 large spring onion,
trimmed and finely sliced

1 red chilli, deseeded
and finely sliced

1 tbsp toasted white sesame seeds

1–2 tsp chilli oil

pinch of dried chilli flakes

½ lime, sliced into wedges

This is one of my favourite recipes. Packed full of flavour, it is perfect for an Earth day snack as it's plant based with a low carbon footprint and it's easy to put together in minutes! The flavours are spicy, nutty, tangy and sweet – so good!

Place all the ingredients for the peanut sauce in a large serving bowl and stir to mix well.

Bring a pan of water to the boil. Add the noodles and cook according to the packet instructions. Drain in cold running water to get rid of the excess starch. Dress the noodles with sesame oil.

Tip the noodles into the sauce and toss to mix well.

Garnish with the coriander, spring onion, fresh chilli and toasted sesame seeds. Finally drizzle over the chilli oil, sprinkle over the dried chilli flakes and toss again. Serve immediately with the lime wedges alongside so you can squeeze them over before eating.

20 mins 15 mins

Malaysian-Style Smoked Mackerel with Egg Laksa Curry

Serves 2

For the laksa paste

1 tsp ground coriander

1 tsp ground cumin

1 tsp ground turmeric

½ onion

40ml (1½fl oz) coconut milk

2.5cm (1in) piece of fresh root ginger, peeled and finely grated

2 garlic cloves

15g (½oz) lemongrass

1 red chilli, deseeded

1 tbsp shrimp paste

For the curry

2 eggs

200g (7oz) smoked mackerel fillets

1 tbsp rapeseed oil

1 small shallot, diced

225g (8oz) French beans, trimmed and sliced in half

250g (9oz) red peppers, cored, deseeded and chopped to 2.5cm (1in) chunks

400ml (14fl oz) coconut milk

400ml (14fl oz) chicken stock

juice of 1 lime

1 tbsp golden syrup

1 tbsp fish sauce

To serve

200g (7oz) cooked egg noodles

2 handfuls of beansprouts

20g (¾oz) fresh coriander

pinch of dried chilli flakes

½ lime, sliced into 2

Based on the Malaysian curry laksa – a coconut curry soup where a spicy curry paste is made from ground spices such as cumin, coriander and turmeric and fused with lemongrass, chillies and onions, and is then cooked with other ingredients in coconut milk, giving a pungent salty, fishy, spicy and sour broth. There are many different types of laksa, and inspired by asam laksa and kedah laksa, here I use smoked mackerel and sliced boiled eggs, which are the perfect accompaniments for this curry broth and will give you a taste of this popular street-food snack from Malaysia. You can use shop-bought laksa paste to cut down on the time as well as budget, if you like. Use cooked egg noodles to make this recipe even quicker.

Preheat the oven to 180°C (350°F), Gas Mark 4.

Put all the ingredients for the laksa paste into a blender or food processor and blitz to a smooth paste. Set aside.

Fill a small pan with water, add the 2 eggs and bring to the boil. Simmer for 3 minutes. Remove the eggs and rinse under cold running water, then crack the shells, peel them off and slice each boiled egg in half down the middle. Set aside.

Place the smoked mackerel fillets on a roasting tray and cook in the oven for 5 minutes until hot. Turn the oven temperature down low and keep warm in the oven.

Heat a large wok over a medium heat until smoking. Add the rapeseed oil and give it a swirl so it coats the sides of the wok. Add the shallot and stir-fry for 30 seconds to release its aroma. Add the laksa paste and stir-fry for 1 minute. Add the French beans and stir-fry for 2 minutes. Then add the red pepper and stir-fry for 1 minute. Add the coconut milk, chicken stock, lime juice, golden syrup and fish sauce and bring to a simmer.

Divide the cooked noodles between 2 large serving bowls. Ladle over the laksa broth. Remove the smoked mackerel from the oven and flake one fillet over each bowl, pair with 2 halves of boiled egg in each bowl and garnish with the beansprouts, coriander sprigs, chilli flakes and sliced lime. Serve immediately.

15 mins 5 mins

Chicken & Sweetcorn Chow Mein

Serves 4

For the noodles

250g (9oz) wide wheat-flour
noodles or flat Japanese udon
noodles

1 tsp toasted sesame oil

For the chow mein

2 tbsp rapeseed oil

2 garlic cloves, finely chopped

2.5cm (1in) piece of fresh root
ginger, peeled and finely grated

2 red chillies, deseeded
and finely chopped

200g (7oz) mini chicken fillets, diced

1 tbsp Shaohsing rice wine

340g (12oz) can sweetcorn, drained

1 tsp dark soy sauce

1 tbsp oyster sauce

1–2 tbsp low-sodium light soy sauce

1 tbsp clear rice vinegar

1 tbsp chilli oil

1 tbsp toasted sesame oil

freshly ground black pepper,
to taste

1 spring onion, trimmed and finely
chopped, to serve

When I was growing up, my mum used to make chicken and sweetcorn ban mein. It was like Mum's version of dan dan noodles but 'ban mein' means a dry 'mixed noodle' dish. First stir-fry the chicken and sweetcorn and toss the noodles in, just mixing in well without stir-frying the noodles. This makes a quick and comforting easy dinner using trusted store-cupboard ingredients.

Bring a pan of water to the boil. Add the noodles and cook according to the packet instructions. Drain in cold running water to get rid of the excess starch. Dress the noodles with sesame oil.

Heat a wok over a high heat until smoking. Add the rapeseed oil and give it a swirl. Add the garlic, ginger and chillies and stir-fry for 30 seconds. Add the diced chicken and cook, stirring, for 2–3 minutes until opaque.

Add the rice wine and sweetcorn and toss well together. Add the dark soy sauce, then follow with the noodles. Season with oyster sauce, light soy sauce, clear rice vinegar, chilli oil, toasted sesame oil and black pepper. Remove from the heat.

Scatter over the spring onion and serve immediately.

Vegan Option   Use minced
soy pieces or diced smoked
tofu instead of chicken and
mushroom sauce instead
of oyster sauce

Wok For Less

5 mins
+
20 mins
marinating
(optional)

35
mins

Hoisin Chicken Beansprout Noodles

Serves 2

2 skin-on chicken drumsticks

2 skin-on chicken thighs

1 spring onion, trimmed and finely sliced, to garnish

For the marinade

2 tbsp hoisin sauce

2.5cm (1in) piece of fresh root ginger, peeled and finely grated

1 tbsp Shaohsing rice wine

2 tbsp low-sodium light soy sauce

1 tbsp dark soy sauce

1 tbsp golden syrup

1 tsp rapeseed oil

For the beansprout noodles

1 tbsp rapeseed oil

2 garlic cloves, crushed

2 spring onions, trimmed and finely chopped

200g (7oz) cooked egg noodles

300g (10½oz) beansprouts

2 tbsp low-sodium light soy sauce

1 tsp toasted sesame oil

large pinch of ground white pepper

I love this easy recipe – perfect for a speedy mid-week supper. Coat some chicken thighs and drumsticks in a rich, savoury-and-sweet hoisin marinade, roast in the oven until sticky and golden and serve with quick beansprout noodles.

Preheat the oven to 180°C (350°F), Gas Mark 4.

Place all the marinade ingredients in a large bowl, add the chicken pieces and toss in the marinade to coat. Cover the bowl with a plate and place in the refrigerator to marinate for 20 minutes. Alternatively, if you don't have time, you can just cook them straight away.

Remove the chicken pieces from the marinade and place in a roasting tray. Roast in the oven for 30 minutes or until cooked all the way through and crispy on top. Remove from the oven and set aside to rest while you make the beansprout noodles.

Heat a wok over a medium heat until smoking. Add the rapeseed oil and give it a swirl. Add the garlic, spring onions, cooked egg noodles, beansprouts and soy sauce, and toss together for 10 seconds. Drizzle with the toasted sesame oil and season with the ground white pepper. Serve immediately with the chicken and garnish with the spring onion.

Vegan Option   Use diced smoked tofu cubes instead of the chicken

5 mins

8 mins

Chicken Pad Thai with Crunchy Veggie Noodles

Serves 2

For the noodles

200g (7oz) flat rice noodles

1 tsp toasted sesame oil

For the chicken

300g (10½oz) chicken breast, sliced into strips

1 tbsp dark soy sauce

1 tbsp cornflour

pinch of sea salt

pinch of ground white pepper

1 tbsp rapeseed oil

2.5cm (1in) piece of fresh root ginger, peeled and finely grated

1 tbsp Shaohsing rice wine

1 tbsp dark soy sauce

200g (7oz) bag of mixed stir-fry vegetables (beansprouts, cabbage, red onion and carrots)

2 small spring onions, trimmed and sliced into 2.5cm (1in) pieces on the diagonal

1–2 tbsp oyster sauce

1 tbsp golden syrup

1–2 tbsp low-sodium light soy sauce or fish sauce

½ lime, juice of

To garnish

50g (1¾oz) roasted, salted peanuts, crushed

pinch of dried chilli flakes

Pad Thai is a traditional stir-fried Thai noodle dish. My tasty version is perfect for a light supper. Use shop-bought veggies and cooked noodles to make the meal even speedier. This recipe is healthy and light without breaking the bank as it uses store-cupboard ingredients.

Bring a pan of water to the boil. Add the flat rice noodles and cook according to the packet instructions. Drain, refresh under cold water and drizzle over the toasted sesame oil. Set aside.

Place the chicken strips in a bowl. Add the dark soy sauce and mix well, add the salt and ground white pepper and then dust with the cornflour.

Heat a large wok over a high heat. Add the rapeseed oil and give it a swirl to coat the sides of the wok. Add the grated ginger and stir for a few seconds to release its flavour and aroma in the oil. Follow with the chicken and stir-fry for 1–2 minutes. Add the rice wine and dark soy sauce and cook for a further minute until the chicken is cooked through.

Quickly follow with the crunchy mixed vegetables and spring onions and toss for 1 minute. Add the oyster sauce, golden syrup, light soy or fish sauce and lime juice. Follow quickly with the cooked rice noodles and toss well together. Cook for another minute until all the ingredients are coated well in the sauce.

To serve, divide the noodles between 2 serving plates, garnish with the peanuts and chilli flakes and eat immediately.

Vegan Option Use slices of shiitake mushrooms or smoked tofu instead of the chicken and mushroom sauce instead of oyster sauce

15 mins · 25 mins

Bang Bang Chicken Peanut Noodles

Serves 2

For the chicken

500ml (18fl oz) water

2 skinless chicken thighs

2 × 1cm (½in) slices of peeled fresh root ginger

1 tbsp Shaohsing rice wine or dry sherry

1 spring onion, trimmed and sliced

½ tsp salt

For the noodles

500ml (18fl oz) water

250g (9oz) cooked thin wheat-flour noodles

1 tbsp toasted sesame oil

For the peanut sauce

1 tbsp rapeseed oil

½ red onion, diced

½ red chilli, deseeded and finely chopped

3 tbsp crunchy peanut butter

100ml (3½fl oz) hot water

½ tsp vegetable bouillon powder

2 tbsp low-sodium light soy sauce

1 tbsp golden syrup

To serve

½ cucumber, deseeded and sliced into half-moons

1 spring onion, trimmed and sliced lengthways

a few sprigs of fresh coriander

1 large handful of roasted, unsalted cashew nuts, chopped

 Vegan Option Use strips of oyster mushroom instead of chicken

This dish originally comes from Sichuan 'bung bung ji', where the chicken meat is tenderized with a 'bung' (a stick) then shredded and mixed with a nutty, soy umami-style sauce, topped with fresh cucumber and served on thin wheat-flour noodles. Street vendors used to sometimes carry bamboo buckets of this dish on poles and bring them to customers. Delicious, simple and reminiscent of a time past with humble and honest ingredients but full of flavour.

Pour the measured water into a wok or pan, then bring to a simmer. Add the chicken thighs, ginger, Shaohsing rice wine, spring onion and salt. Simmer over a gentle heat for 20 minutes.

Lift out the spring onion and discard. Remove the chicken thighs carefully with a slotted spoon and transfer to a chopping board, then shred the meat. Throw the bones back into the stock and keep it covered in the fridge for another recipe. Set the shredded chicken thigh meat to one side.

In a medium pan, bring the measured water to the boil. Add the noodles and cook according to the packet instructions. Drain and rinse under cold water. Drizzle over the toasted sesame oil and set aside.

To make the peanut sauce, heat a wok over a medium heat until smoking. Add the rapeseed oil and give it a swirl. Add the red onion and red chilli and fry for 1–2 minutes until golden. Add the "peanut butter, measured hot water and bouillon powder and whisk until mixed well. Season with the light soy sauce and golden syrup and bring to a simmer to fuse the flavours of the sauce.

Remove and transfer to a serving dish. Leave it for 5 minutes to cool to room temperature.

Divide the noodles between 2 plates, garnish with the cucumber slices, top with the chicken, drizzle over the peanut sauce, then top with the spring onion, coriander and roasted cashew nuts. Serve immediately.

10 mins 10 mins

Hakka Pork Mee

Serves 2

For the sauce

1 tbsp dark soy sauce

2 tbsp low-sodium light soy sauce

1 tbsp oyster sauce

1 tsp chilli bean sauce

100ml (3½fl oz) vegetable stock

1 tsp cornflour

1 tbsp cold water

For the noodles

200g (7oz) thin egg noodles

1 tbsp toasted sesame oil

For the pork

1 tbsp rapeseed oil

2 garlic cloves, finely chopped

2.5cm (1in) piece of fresh root
ginger, roughly chopped

1 red chilli, deseeded
and roughly chopped

¼ red onion, diced

200g (7oz) minced lean pork

1 large carrot, trimmed
and finely diced

1 courgette, trimmed
and finely diced

1 tbsp Shaohsing rice wine

To serve

1 spring onion, trimmed
and finely sliced

1 red chilli, deseeded
and finely sliced

1 tbsp clear rice vinegar

2 garlic cloves, grated

2 tbsp of your favourite chilli
sauce

I first tried this delicious Malaysian dish in my husband's family town of Ipoh. It was made with minced pork served on thin egg noodles enveloped in an aromatic oniony, savoury flavour. It's a dry noodle dish full of punchy garlicky tastes. This is my version. Enjoy!

In a jug, mix the dark soy sauce, light soy sauce, oyster sauce, chilli bean sauce, vegetable stock, cornflour and measured cold water to combine the flavours.

Bring a pan of water to the boil. Add the noodles and cook according to the packet instructions. Drain, refresh under cold water and drizzle over the toasted sesame oil. Set aside.

Heat a wok over a high heat until smoking, then add the rapeseed oil and give it a swirl. Add the garlic, ginger, chilli and red onion and stir-fry for a few seconds to release their aroma.

Add the minced pork, break it apart and stir-fry for 1–2 minutes. Add the carrot and courgette and stir-fry together for 2–3 minutes, adding a few drops of water to create some steam. Cook for another 1 minute, then season with the Shaohsing rice wine.

Pour in the sauce, then stir to thicken. Spoon the mixture over the egg noodles. Garnish with the finely chopped spring onion and serve immediately with the sliced red chillies dressed in the vinegar and grated garlic mixed with your favourite chilli sauce on the side.

15 mins 5 mins

Saucy Oyster Sauce Beef & Broccoli Chow Mein

Serves 2

For the beef

180g (6⅓oz) beef rump fillet, diced

¼ tsp bicarbonate of soda

2.5cm (1in) piece of fresh root ginger, peeled and finely grated

1 tbsp oyster sauce

1 tbsp low-sodium light soy sauce

2 pinches of ground white pepper

1 tbsp cornflour

For the chow mein

350ml (14fl oz) water

200g (7oz) long-stem broccoli, cut into bite-sized pieces

2 tbsp rapeseed oil

200g (7oz) cooked egg noodles

pinch of ground black pepper

1 spring onion, trimmed and finely sliced, to garnish

For the seasoning

2 tbsp oyster sauce

1 tbsp low-sodium light soy sauce

200ml (7fl oz) cold vegetable stock

2 tbsp cornflour

Nothing beats a classic beef and oyster sauce broccoli chow mein – the combination of juicy beef rump steak tossed in an umami oyster sauce with tender broccoli steams on chunky egg noodles and seasoned with big hits of ground black pepper makes this an all-round winner. Instead of the drier versions of this classic, I've made it saucier to coat the delicious noodles. Enjoy!

In a jug, add all the seasoning ingredients and stir to combine well. In a bowl add the beef pieces, bicarbonate of soda, ginger, oyster sauce, light soy sauce, ground white pepper and cornflour. Mix to coat well and let it marinate for 10 minutes.

Pour the measured water into a wok, then bring to the boil. Add the broccoli pieces and blanch for 30 seconds. Remove, then drain.

Reheat the wok over a high heat until smoking. Add the rapeseed oil and give it a swirl. Add the marinated beef and let it settle for 30 seconds, then toss and stir-fry for 5 seconds to sear and colour the edges. For medium done, cook for another 20 seconds. Add the sauce, bring to the boil and cook for 3–4 minutes until thickened enough to coat the beef.

Add the broccoli and cooked egg noodles. Toss together well, stirring everything thoroughly. Add the ground black pepper, sprinkle over the spring onion and serve immediately.

Vegan Option   Add some chunky king trumpet mushrooms sliced into 5cm (2in) batons, mushroom sauce instead of oyster sauce and wheat-flour noodles instead of egg noodles

Wok For Less

5 mins   10 mins

Japanese Teriyaki Beef Udon Noodle Stir-Fry

Serves 2

For the noodles

250g (9oz) udon noodles

1 tsp toasted sesame oil

For the beef

1 × 200g (7oz) grass-fed or British ribeye beef steak excess fat trimmed off, sliced 1.5cm (¾in) thick

1 tbsp dark soy sauce

1 tbsp cornflour

For the stir-fry

1 tbsp rapeseed oil

2 garlic cloves, finely chopped

2 tbsp mirin

2 tbsp low-sodium light soy sauce

1 tbsp golden syrup

200g (7oz) bag of mixed stir-fry vegetables (beansprouts, cabbage, red onion and carrots)

1 tbsp Shaohsing rice wine

dash of toasted sesame oil (optional)

To garnish

2 spring onions, trimmed and sliced into 2.5cm (1in) pieces on the diagonal, or cut into long strips and placed in ice water to curl (optional)

Teriyaki is a cooking technique in which ingredients are covered in a glaze of soy, mirin and sugar and then grilled. This cooking technique is now popularly known as a flavour profile in its own right. The smoky, sweet, soy flavour is delicious paired with most meats and fish, but the ultimate pairing is with beef strips in a delicious noodle stir-fry with chunky udon noodles – and maybe a glass of plummy Shiraz or Zinfandel.

Bring a pan of water to the boil. Add the udon noodles and cook according to the packet instructions. Drain, run under cold water, drain again, then drizzle over the toasted sesame oil.

Place the beef in a bowl. Add the dark soy sauce and mix well, then dust with the cornflour.

Heat a large wok over a high heat until smoking. Add the rapeseed oil and give it a swirl around to coat the wok. Add the garlic and stir-fry for a few seconds to release its aroma. Add the beef, let it sit for about 10 seconds to brown the edges, then turn and toss for 20–30 seconds to brown it all over.

Season the beef with the mirin, 1 tablespoon of the light soy sauce and the golden syrup, then toss to caramelize. Add the mixed vegetables and stir-fry for 1 minute.

Add the Shaohsing rice wine, then add the cooked udon noodles and toss together well.

Season with the remaining tablespoon of light soy sauce and the toasted sesame oil, if using. Garnish with the spring onions for a fresh bite. Divide the dish between 2 plates to serve and eat immediately.

Vegan Option   Use chunky slices of oyster mushrooms or smoked tofu instead of the beef

5 mins 10 mins

Smoked Bacon Chow Mein

Serves 2

1 tbsp rapeseed oil

200g (7oz) smoked bacon lardons

1 tsp dark soy sauce

100g (3½oz) red peppers, cored, deseeded and sliced into julienne strips

100g (3½oz) mangetout, sliced into julienne strips

1 tbsp Shaohsing rice wine

200g (7oz) cooked egg noodles

1 tbsp oyster sauce

1 tbsp low-sodium light soy sauce

1 tsp toasted sesame oil

100g (3½oz) beansprouts

To garnish

pinch of dried chilli flakes

1 spring onion, trimmed and sliced

'Chow' in Mandarin Chinese means 'to stir' and 'mein' means 'noodle', so 'stir-fried noodle'. This is a popular Chinese restaurant and takeaway dish and is extremely versatile. Smoked bacon lardons are inexpensive but a tasty choice for a speedy, delish supper.

Heat a large wok over a high heat until slightly smoking. Add the rapeseed oil and give it a swirl. Add the smoked bacon lardons and fry for 1–2 minutes until crispy.

Add the dark soy sauce, then the red peppers and mangetout and toss for 1 minute. Season with the Shaohsing rice wine. Add the egg noodles, then toss and stir so all the flavours are combined well.

Add the oyster sauce, light soy sauce and toasted sesame oil, then the beansprouts. Toss well for 1–2 minutes. Garnish with the chilli flakes and spring onions, then serve and eat immediately.

 Vegan Option   Use diced smoked tofu pieces, shiitake mushrooms or tempeh cubes instead of the bacon lardons, mushroom sauce instead of oyster sauce and wheat-flour noodles instead of egg noodles

Fast, Fresh, Flavourful Noodles

4.

Entertaining, Sharing & Leftover Meals

4

Entertaining, Sharing & Leftover Meals

Next up, this chapter looks at recipes that can be easily doubled up for cooking for family and friends, plus those that can be turned into another meal the next day – so many possibilities can stem from one dish. This chapter is really dedicated to families and family occasions, with recipes that can be multiplied for a family-style buffet to be laid at the centre of the table. But they can also be made as a simple meal for two that, with clever use of leftovers, you can turn into an easy meal the next day.

Cooking in this way saves time and money, and the recipes in this chapter are super versatile: my Chilli Beef Brisket (see page 148) can be shredded and made into Chilli Beef Brisket Baos or Beef Brisket Noodles (see pages 152 and 150). Or my aromatic Hoisin Roast Duck Legs (see page 136) can be turned into Roast Duck Lettuce Cups or Roast Duck Noodles (see pages 140 and 138). Or any chicken bones left from making Roast Chilli Chicken, Mouth-watering Chicken or Easy Hainan Chicken Rice (see pages 128, 126 and 132) can be used to make my Next Day Rainbow Chicken Bone Broth with Shiitake Mushrooms (see page 127). Likewise, any leftovers from my Soy Butter Roast Chicken (see page 116) can be used to make Leftover Soy Butter Chicken Fried Lettuce with Hazelnuts or my Leftover Soy Butter Chicken Spring Onion Chow Mein (see pages 118 and 120).

Not all of the recipes in this chapter can be turned into leftover meals, but if you increase the quantities of those that can't, they will certainly keep until the next day so you can get two meals for the effort and price of one.

15 mins

8 mins

Yusiang Aubergine with French Beans

Serves 2 or 4 to share

For the sauce

200ml (7fl oz) cold vegetable stock

2 tbsp rice vinegar

2 tbsp low-sodium light soy sauce

1 tbsp toasted sesame oil

1 tbsp golden syrup

1 tbsp cornflour

2 tbsp rapeseed oil

300g (10½oz) aubergine, trimmed and sliced into quarters lengthways, then into chunky 2cm x 6cm (¾in x 2½in) finger strips

100ml (3½fl oz) x 2 cold water

1 tsp whole toasted Sichuan peppercorns (optional)

2 garlic cloves, finely chopped

2.5cm (1in) piece of fresh root ginger, peeled and finely grated

1 red chilli, deseeded and finely chopped

100g (3½oz) French beans, trimmed and sliced into 4cm (1½in) pieces

1 tsp dark soy sauce

1 tsp chilli bean paste

1 tbsp Shaohsing rice wine or dry sherry

2 spring onions, trimmed and sliced into 0.5cm (¼in) rounds, to garnish

cooked jasmine rice (see page 22), to serve

This recipe is an adaptation of one of my favourite Sichuan dishes. It does not contain any fish but is called 'fish fragrant', or 'yusiang', because it uses a good savoury stock. Use minced soy or shiitake mushrooms and serve it with steamed jasmine rice. It's delish and packs a punch. For a 'saucier' dish you can increase the amount of sauce. This is a super satisfying and warming dish.

Place all the ingredients for the sauce in a jug. Stir well and set aside until needed.

Heat a wok over a high heat until smoking. Add 1 tablespoon of the rapeseed oil and give it a swirl. Add the aubergine pieces and cook, stirring, for 5 minutes, until browned. As you cook it, frequently add drops of the measured water, up to 100ml (3½fl oz) in total, to create steam to help soften the aubergine (this is much healthier than frying it in lots of oil). Repeat this with the other 100ml (3½fl oz) of water until the aubergine has softened.

Push the aubergine to the far side of the wok. Add the remaining tablespoon of rapeseed oil. Add the Sichuan peppercorns, if using, garlic, ginger and chilli. Stir-fry for a few seconds, and then toss with the aubergine. Add the French beans, then season with the dark soy sauce, chilli bean paste and Shaohsing rice wine.

Pour over the sauce and bring to the boil, cooking for 1 minute, or until the sauce thickens. Give it a final mix, then remove from the heat.

Sprinkle over the spring onions and serve immediately with jasmine rice.

10 mins   15 mins

Shiitake Mushroom Stir-Fry on Steamed Tofu

Serves 2 or 4 to share

For the tofu

400g (14oz) block of soft tofu, drained

1 tbsp Shaohsing rice wine

pinch of sea salt

pinch of ground white pepper

2 spring onions, trimmed and sliced into 1cm (½in) rounds, to garnish

cooked jasmine rice (see page 22), to serve

For the mushrooms

1 tbsp rapeseed oil

2 garlic cloves, finely chopped

2.5cm (1in) piece of fresh root ginger, peeled and finely grated

200g (7oz) fresh shiitake mushrooms, sliced

For the sauce

2 tbsp clear rice vinegar

1 tbsp toasted sesame oil

2 tbsp low-sodium light soy sauce

2 tbsp vegetarian mushroom sauce

200ml (7fl oz) cold vegetable stock

3 tbsp cornflour

I first had freshly made tofu in Huang Lo farm restaurant outside of Shanghai. It was perhaps the best freshly made tofu I'd ever had: silky, beany, fresh and wobbly and soft. The restaurant served an array of condiments to go with the dish and I was in tofu heaven. Inspired by that dish, here I steam the tofu and make a savoury mushroom stir-fry to pour on the tofu for maximum taste.

Slice the tofu into 1.5cm (¾in) cubes but keep it as a complete block, then transfer to a heatproof plate. Season the tofu with the Shaohsing rice wine, salt and ground white pepper. Place the plate on a steamer rack in a wok filled with water. Cover with a tight-fitting lid, bring the water to the boil and steam over a medium heat for 8 minutes.

Meanwhile, mix together all the sauce ingredients in a bowl.

Heat a wok over a high heat until smoking. Add the rapeseed oil and give it a swirl. Add the garlic and ginger and allow them to sizzle for a few seconds before adding the shiitake mushrooms. Cook for 1 minute.

Add the sauce, bring to the boil, then take off the heat and set aside.

Remove the steamed tofu, plate and all, from the steamer. Pour over the mushrooms, garnish with spring onions, and serve immediately with cooked jasmine rice.

15 mins 6–7 mins

Spicy Prawns x Ketchup Fried Rice

Serves 2

1 tbsp rapeseed oil

1 white onion, diced

10 tiger prawns, shelled, deveined and sliced in half down the middle

1 tbsp Shaohsing rice wine

½ tsp dark soy sauce

½ tsp chilli bean sauce

2 tbsp tomato ketchup

300g (10½oz) cooked jasmine rice (see page 22)

225g (8oz) can water chestnuts, drained, or 140g (5oz) defrosted peas

1–2 tbsp low-sodium light soy sauce

1 tsp rice vinegar

dash of toasted sesame oil

pinch of ground white pepper

1 spring onion, trimmed and finely sliced, to garnish

My mum used to make ketchup fried rice for us when we were growing up, and it was a dish we always looked forward to. The tangy ketchup with a slight hint of chilli from the chilli bean paste and the crunchy sweet water chestnuts make this dish super delicious and addictive. You will not be disappointed.

Heat a wok over a medium heat until smoking. Add the rapeseed oil and give it a swirl. Add the onion and tiger prawns and toss for 5 seconds. Season with the Shaohsing rice wine, dark soy sauce, chilli bean sauce and 1 tablespoon of the ketchup and toss for 2 seconds to coat well.

Before the prawns turn completely pink, add the cooked jasmine rice and, using the wooden spoon or metal spatula, start to gently break apart the rice grains: not in a stabbing motion but just tossing the ingredients well for 1–2 minutes.

Add the water chestnuts or peas and toss well. Season with the light soy sauce, remaining tablespoon of ketchup and the rice vinegar, toasted sesame oil and ground white pepper. Toss well. Garnish with the spring onion and serve immediately.

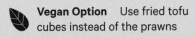

Vegan Option Use fried tofu cubes instead of the prawns

15 mins   8 mins

Black Bean Tofu & Baby Pak Choi

Serves 2 or 4 to share

For the pak choy

90g (3oz) baby pak choy, halved

pinch of sea salt

1 tbsp Shaohsing rice wine

1 tbsp low-sodium light soy sauce

1 tsp toasted sesame oil

2.5cm (1in) piece of fresh root ginger, peeled and sliced into matchsticks

For the black bean tofu

1 tbsp cornflour

2 tbsp cold water

1 tbsp rapeseed oil

5 garlic cloves, finely chopped

2.5cm (1in) piece of fresh root ginger, peeled and finely grated

1 red chilli, deseeded and chopped

1 bird's eye chilli, deseeded and chopped

1 tbsp fermented salted black beans, rinsed and crushed, or black bean sauce

1 tbsp miso paste or yellow bean sauce

150g (5½oz) ready-fried tofu pieces (or regular tofu, frozen overnight and defrosted – see recipe intro), quartered

1 tbsp Shaohsing rice wine or dry sherry

3 baby courgettes, sliced into 1cm (½in) thick rounds

200ml (7fl oz) vegetable stock

1 tbsp low-sodium light soy sauce

cooked jasmine rice (see page 22), to serve

I love the flavour of fermented salted black beans and this is one of my favourite easy suppers. Black bean sauce, white onions, green peppers and chilli are a winning combination; whether you pair it with beef or serve with ready-fried tofu, it's super delicious. If you can't get ready-fried tofu, freeze a block of tofu (the kind that is in a block of 'water') overnight, then defrost before use; the water crystals will produce large 'pores' in the tofu that make it extra 'spongy', helping it absorb the delicious umami flavours of the rich sauce. If you can't get fermented salted black beans, buy a good-quality black bean sauce instead.

Place a heatproof plate inside a bamboo steamer. Season the pak choy with the salt, rice wine, light soy sauce and toasted sesame oil, then lay the ginger slices over the top. Place the lid on the steamer and set over a wok or pan of water. Bring to the boil, then gently steam over a low heat for 3–4 minutes. Turn off the heat and keep warm in the steamer until ready to serve.

In a small jug or cup, mix the cornflour with the measured water to create a slurry. Set aside until needed.

While the pak choy is steaming, place a wok over a high heat. Add the rapeseed oil and give it a swirl. When the oil starts to smoke, add the garlic, ginger and both chillies and stir-fry for a few seconds. Then add the black beans or black bean sauce and miso paste or yellow bean sauce and quickly stir.

Add the tofu and stir-fry for 1 minute, keeping the ingredients moving in the wok, then add the rice wine or sherry and the baby courgettes and stir-fry for a further minute.

Add the stock and then bring to the boil. Season with the soy sauce, then add the cornflour slurry and stir to thicken.

Serve the black bean tofu and steamed baby pak choy with jasmine rice on the side and eat immediately.

15 mins

8 mins

Crispy Spicy Garlic Tofu with Chinese Leaf

Serves 2 or 4 to share

200g (7oz) block of fresh firm tofu, drained and sliced into 1.5cm (¾in) cubes

pinch of sea salt

pinch of ground white pepper

2 tbsp cornflour

3–4 tbsp rapeseed oil

2 garlic cloves, finely chopped

2.5cm (1in) piece of fresh root ginger, peeled and finely grated

½ Chinese leaf, sliced in half lengthways and cut into 1–2.5cm (½–1in) slices

1 tbsp Shaohsing rice wine or dry sherry

1 tbsp chilli bean sauce

225g (8oz) can water chestnuts, drained and sliced

1 tbsp low-sodium light soy sauce

1 tbsp golden syrup

cooked jasmine rice (see page 22), to serve

To garnish

3 spring onions, trimmed and sliced into 1cm (½in) rounds on a deep angle

1 small handful of roasted, unsalted cashew nuts

Fresh tender Chinese leaf is sliced and tossed in a sweetened spicy chilli bean sauce, dressed with umami light soy sauce, and mixed with nutty water chestnuts, crispy golden fried tofu, spring onions and cashew nuts. The spicy sauce delivers a garlicky kick to the tofu and the Chinese leaf, imparting the dish with a slight red hue, and the soy gives a salty fresh pop – enjoy!

Place the tofu cubes in a deep bowl. Season them with the salt and ground white pepper, dust over the cornflour and toss well to coat.

Heat a wok over a high heat until smoking. Add 2–3 tablespoons of the rapeseed oil and give it a swirl. Add the tofu cubes and fry on all sides for 3–4 minutes until they turn golden and crispy. Remove and set aside.

Reheat the wok over a high heat until smoking, add the remaining tablespoon of rapeseed oil and give it a swirl. Add the garlic and ginger and stir for a few seconds, then add the Chinese leaf and toss and stir-fry for 2 minutes until tender.

Season with the Shaohsing rice wine or dry sherry, then add the chilli bean sauce, followed by the water chestnuts. Toss for a few seconds to combine and coat the ingredients well, then season with the light soy sauce and golden syrup.

Add the crispy golden tofu back into the wok and toss for 30 seconds.

Garnish with the spring onions and cashew nuts. To serve, transfer to a plate and serve immediately with jasmine rice.

10 mins

5 mins

Kung Pao Tofu

Serves 2

400g (14oz) fresh or shop-bought ready-fried firm tofu, drained and sliced into 2cm (1in) cubes

pinch of salt

pinch of ground white pepper

1 tbsp cornflour

3 tbsp rapeseed oil

2 garlic cloves, finely chopped

2.5cm (1in) piece of fresh root ginger, peeled and finely grated

5 fresh shiitake mushrooms, sliced into 1cm (½in) slices

225g (8oz) can water chestnuts, drained and sliced

1 tbsp Shaohsing rice wine

cooked jasmine rice (see page 22), to serve

For the sauce

150ml (5fl oz) cold vegetable stock

1 tsp chilli bean sauce

1 tbsp low-sodium light soy sauce

½ tsp dark soy sauce

1 tbsp cornflour

To garnish

10g (¼oz) chopped chives

pinch of dried chilli flakes

Here tofu is enhanced by multi-layered Chinese flavours, including a taste-packed kung pao sauce and Shaohsing rice wine. The combination of earthy mushrooms and crunchy water chestnuts makes this a true vegan winner. Topped with chives and dried chilli flakes, this dish's textures and layers of flavours are truly unique. It's perfect on its own, with plain rice and pickles on the side, or as a hot topping on a bibimbap dish or hot poke bowl, like an East–East veggie mashup.

If using fresh tofu, season the tofu cubes with the salt and ground white pepper. Dip the tofu cubes in the cornflour. Heat a wok over a high heat until slightly smoking. Add 2 tablespoons of the rapeseed oil and give it a swirl. Add the tofu and fry on all sides for a few minutes until it is golden and has a slightly crisp texture. Remove and set aside.

In a small bowl, mix together the sauce ingredients, then set aside.

Wash out the wok, then reheat over a high heat until slightly smoking. Add the remaining tablespoon of the rapeseed oil. Add the garlic and ginger and fry for a few seconds, then add the mushrooms and water chestnuts. Stir-fry for 1 minute until brown, then add the Shaohsing rice wine.

Add the sauce, and cook, stirring, for 1 minute, or until the sauce has thickened and coats all the ingredients well. Add the crispy tofu back into the pan and toss well to coat the tofu.

Garnish with the chopped chives and chilli flakes, then serve immediately with jasmine rice.

10 mins 5–6 mins

Mapo Tofu, Mushrooms, Peas & Bamboo Shoots

Serves 2 or 4 to share

1–2 tbsp groundnut oil

2 garlic cloves, finely chopped

2.5cm (1in) piece of fresh root ginger, peeled and grated

1 red chilli, deseeded and finely chopped

1 tbsp chilli bean paste

1 small handful of fresh shiitake mushrooms

120g (4½oz) frozen peas

120g (4½oz) canned bamboo shoots, cut into julienne strips

400g (14oz) fresh firm tofu, drained and sliced into 1.5cm (½in) cubes

1 tbsp Shaohsing rice wine or dry sherry

1 tbsp low-sodium light soy sauce

1 tbsp clear rice vinegar

200ml (7fl oz) cold vegetable stock

1 tbsp Sichuan preserved vegetables in chilli oil, finely chopped (optional)

1 tbsp cornflour, blended with 2 tbsp cold water

salt and freshly ground pepper, to taste

To serve

cooked jasmine rice (see page 22)

2 pinches of ground toasted Sichuan peppercorns

1 spring onion, trimmed and finely sliced

1 small bunch of fresh coriander, leaves picked and stems chopped

chilli oil (optional)

Spicy mapo tofu was invented by Mrs Chen, a Sichuan street hawker who put both the dish and the city of Chengdu on the culinary map! The classic version includes some minced pork and Sichuan preserved vegetables for that sour briny taste, which is a delightfully classic addition but totally optional. I use tofu and have also added peas for a sweet, modern vegan take. Perfect with jasmine rice for the ultimate comfort food.

Heat a wok over a high heat until smoking. Add the rapeseed oil and give it a swirl. Add the garlic, ginger and chilli. Cook, stirring, for a few seconds, before adding the chilli bean paste, followed by the skiitake mushrooms, frozen peas, bamboo shoots and tofu. Cook, tossing, for 10 seconds.

Add the Shaohsing rice wine or sherry, light soy sauce, vinegar and stock, and bring to a simmer. Stir in the Sichuan preserved vegetables, if using, and blended cornflour. Season to taste with the saltand freshly ground pepper.

Serve immediately with jasmine rice, garnished with the ground toasted Sichuan peppercorns, spring onion and coriander stems and leaves. Drizzle with extra chilli oil if you wish.

15 mins

7 mins

Three Cup Tofu

Serves 2 or 4 to share

1 tbsp rapeseed oil

2.5cm (1in) piece of fresh root ginger, peeled and cut into large slices

2 garlic cloves, crushed but left whole

1 red chilli, deseeded and sliced into rings

300g (10½oz) deep-fried tofu, cut into 2.5cm (1in) cubes and rinsed

1 tbsp Shaohsing rice wine

50ml (2fl oz) low-sodium light soy sauce

50ml (2fl oz) toasted sesame oil

1 tbsp golden syrup

5g (⅛oz) Thai sweet basil

cooked jasmine rice
(see page 22), to serve

This classic Taiwanese dish is warm and comforting – perfect for cold weather. The tofu, ginger and chilli will give you a warm zingy lift. It's also speedy – prepared in 5 minutes and cooked in 7 – which means chopping board to table in under 15 minutes. Traditionally the dish uses 1 cup of soy sauce, 1 cup of rice wine and 1 cup of toasted sesame oil; there's not a whole cup of each in this recipe but it still uses all three ingredients for maximum flavour. If Japan is famous for inventing their teriyaki sauce, Taiwan is famous for inventing three cup sauce. The basil at the end imparts a sweet aniseed aroma and taste, which pairs perfectly with the dish. In Taiwan nine pagoda basil, a unique herb, is the secret key to this dish.

Heat a wok over a high heat until smoking. Add the rapeseed oil and give it a swirl. Add the ginger slices and fry for 8 seconds until crispy and golden, then add the garlic and red chilli and toss for a few seconds to release their flavour.

Add the tofu pieces and leave for a few seconds to sear and colour on one side, then flip them over and sear on the other side. Season with the Shaohsing rice wine and stir-fry for another 10 seconds.

Add the light soy sauce, toasted sesame oil and golden syrup and cook for 5 minutes until the liquid has almost evaporated. The tofu should be slightly caramelized at the edges, a little darker brown, and have a slightly sticky shine.

Add the basil leaves and toss through to wilt, then take off the heat and serve immediately with jasmine rice.

Wok For Less

10 mins   10 mins

Steamed Cod in Chilli Bean Sauce

Serves 2

400g (14oz) skinless cod fillets

pinch of salt

pinch of ground white pepper

1 tbsp Shaohsing rice wine

1 tbsp cornflour, blended with 2 tbsp cold water

spring onion curls (see page 88), to garnish

cooked jasmine rice (see page 22), to serve

For the sauce

1 tbsp low-sodium light soy sauce

1 tbsp oyster sauce

1 tsp chilli bean sauce

1 tsp caster sugar

200ml (7fl oz) cold vegetable stock

1 tbsp cornflour

1 tbsp rapeseed oil

2.5cm (1in) piece of fresh root ginger, peeled and sliced into matchsticks

2 red chillies, deseeded and finely chopped

50g (1¾oz) frozen peas

150g (5½oz) shiitake mushrooms, sliced

1 tbsp Shaohsing rice wine

2 large spring onions, trimmed and sliced into 1cm (½in) rounds

The Mandarin word for fish is 'yu', which is the homonym for 'abundance', therefore it is important to have it at Chinese New Year. This meal will bring an abundance of luck, wealth happiness – whatever you wish for! Red is also an auspicious colour and the red chillies bring warmth as well as luck. The umami shiitake mushrooms have an earthy flavour and provide a 'meaty' savouriness. Use premium oyster sauce for a rich savoury note that compliments the cod well.

Place the cod fillets in a deep, heatproof dish that will fit inside a steamer. Season with the salt and white pepper, then pour over the rice wine and blended cornflour.

Set the plate on a steamer set over a wok half-filled with water. Place the lid on the steamer. Bring the water to the boil and steam the cod over a medium heat for 5–6 minutes. Remove from the heat and leave in the steamer to keep warm.

Meanwhile for the sauce, in a small bowl mix together the light soy sauce, oyster sauce, chilli bean sauce, caster sugar, cold vegetable stock and cornflour. Mix well.

Heat a wok over a high heat until smoking. Add the rapeseed oil and give it a swirl. Quickly add the ginger and chillies, stir for a few seconds, then add the frozen peas and sliced shiitake mushrooms and stir-fry for a few seconds. Add the rice wine and stir-fry for another 20 seconds. Pour in the mixed sauces, and then bring to the boil.

Boil for 30 seconds until the sauce thickens, then stir in the spring onions. Remove the fish from the steamer and place on a serving plate. Add any cooking juices from the fish to the sauce and stir in well. Pour the sauce over the fish, then garnish with spring onion curls and serve immediately with jasmine rice.

5 mins 12 min

Oven-Baked Sweet Spicy Salmon with Oyster Sauce Noodles

Serves 2

For the salmon

2 × 120g (4¼oz) pieces of skin-on salmon fillet

2.5cm (1in) piece of fresh root ginger, peeled and finely grated

½ tsp chilli bean sauce

2 tsp Shaohsing rice wine

2 tsp low-sodium light soy sauce

pinch of dried chilli flakes

½ red onion, sliced into half-moons

2 tsp olive or rapeseed oil

2 tsp golden syrup

For the vegetable noodle stir-fry

1 tbsp rapeseed oil

300g (10½oz) pack of rainbow stir-fry vegetables (or a selection of baby pak choy, carrot strips and red pepper)

300g (10½oz) cooked egg noodles

1 tbsp oyster sauce

1–2 tbsp low-sodium light soy sauce

dash of toasted sesame oil

pinch of cracked black pepper

To garnish

finely chopped spring onions or spring onion curls (see page 88)

Salmon fillets are seasoned with chilli bean sauce, Shaohsing rice wine, light soy sauce and dried chilli flakes and baked in the oven for a hearty, healthy meal full of omega-3 fatty acids. Meanwhile a simple stir-fry of vegetables and cooked noodles seasoned with oyster sauce makes this dish delightful to eat.

Preheat the oven to 180°C (350°F), Gas Mark 4.

Place the salmon fillets in a shallow roasting tray. Add all the aromatics from the ginger all the way down to the chilli flakes, then lay the red onion slices on top. Drizzle the olive or rapeseed oil over the fillets. Place the tray in the oven and bake for 10 minutes. Remove from the oven, brush over the golden syrup and return to the oven for 2 minutes to caramelize.

Meanwhile, 5 minutes before the salmon is ready, heat a large wok or pan over a high heat until smoking. Add the rapeseed oil and give it a swirl to coat the sides. Add the pack of stir-fry vegetables and toss to cook for 1 minute.

Add the cooked egg noodles, season with oyster sauce, light soy sauce, toasted sesame oil and black pepper and combine well.

Divide the noodles and vegetables between 4 plates, then remove the salmon from the oven and place on top of each noodle portion. Garnish with spring onions and serve immediately.

15 mins   3–4 mins

Spicy Sweet Oyster Sauce Prawns with Pine Nuts

Serves 2

For the marinade

2.5cm (1in) piece of fresh root ginger, peeled and finely grated

1 tsp organic miso paste

1 tbsp oyster sauce

1 tsp dark soy sauce

8 large tiger prawns, shelled and deveined, shell off, tail on

For the prawns

2 tbsp rapeseed oil

1 garlic clove, crushed

1 red chilli, deseeded and finely chopped

1 tbsp Shaohsing rice wine

1 tbsp low-sodium light soy sauce

1 tbsp golden syrup

To serve

1 handful of toasted pine nuts

2 spring onions, trimmed and finely chopped

1 tsp chilli oil

cooked jasmine rice (see page 22)

This is an all-round Asian fusion dish – the miso, oyster and honey work so well with the sweetness of the prawns. A real mix of umami – the dish is salty, spicy and sweet – which is perfect with Jasmine rice and the nutty pop of toasted pine nuts.

Add all the ingredients for the marinade to a bowl and mix well. Add the prawns and marinate for 15 minutes.

Heat a wok or pan over a high heat and add the rapeseed oil. Add the garlic and chilli and stir-fry for a few seconds to release their aroma. Add the marinated prawns and toss for 2 minutes. Season with the Shaohsing rice wine, light soy sauce and golden syrup. Toss while cooking to caramelise the prawns.

Sprinkle in the pine nuts and the spring onions. Transfer to serving plate, drizzle over the chilli oil and serve immediately with jasmine rice.

15 mins 8 mins

Steamed Seabass in Chilli Bean Sauce

Serves 2 or 4 to share

For the fish

1 whole fresh seabass (head to tail), up to 30cm (12in) long, gutted, cleaned and patted dry

pinch of sea salt

pinch of ground white pepper

2.5cm (1in) piece of fresh root ginger, peeled and sliced into matchsticks

1 tbsp Shaohsing rice wine or dry sherry

1 heaped tbsp cornflour, blended with 2 tbsp cold water

For the chilli bean sauce

1 tbsp chilli bean paste

150ml (5fl oz) cold vegetable stock

1–2 tbsp low-sodium light soy sauce

1 tbsp clear rice vinegar

1 heaped tbsp cornflour

2 tbsp rapeseed oil

2 garlic cloves, finely chopped

2.5cm (1in) piece of fresh root ginger, peeled and finely grated

2 red chillies, deseeded and finely chopped

½ tsp Sichuan pepper, toasted, then ground in a pestle and mortar (optional)

3 spring onions, trimmed and sliced into 1cm (½in) rounds

fresh coriander leaves, to garnish

cooked jasmine rice (see page 22)

1 quantity Easy Garlic or Ginger Pak Choy (see page 180)

 Vegan Option Steam a large block of tofu, pour the sauce over and serve with rice

Ideal for fish lovers, this dish makes a perfect centrepiece for everyone to help themselves. A whole seabass symbolizes abundance, and the reddish colour of the sauce represents bringing lots of luck. If you don't have Sichuan pepper, leave it out: the chilli bean sauce delivers enough umami and spice. To ensure you get a fresh seabass check the eyes are not sunken, there's no unpleasant smell and the skin is silky to the touch. If you can't get seabass, you can use any fish of your choice; cod fillets also work well. You could also use frozen fish – just follow the packet instructions if cooking from frozen to ensure it cooks all the way through.

Place the whole seabass on a deep, heatproof dish that fits inside a steamer. Season both sides with the salt and ground white pepper. Stuff the belly with the ginger matchsticks. Pour over the rice wine or sherry, followed by the blended cornflour.

Set the plate on a steamer set over a wok half-filled with water. Place the lid on the steamer. Bring the water to the boil and steam the seabass over a medium heat for 6–7 minutes (depending on the size of the fish) until the fish is opaque white when poked gently. When the seabass is cooked, turn the heat off and leave in the steamer to keep warm. Set aside.

Meanwhile to make the sauce, in a bowl, mix the chilli bean paste, cold vegetable stock, light soy sauce, clear rice vinegar and cornflour until combined well.

Heat another wok over a high heat until smoking. Add the rapeseed oil and give it a swirl. Add the garlic, ginger, chillies, Sichuan pepper, if using, and spring onions and stir-fry for a few seconds, then add the mixed sauces. Bring to the boil, then reduce the heat to very low. Use a wide whisk to mix the sauce until smooth.

Carefully remove the fish from the steamer and transfer to a serving plate. Add any remaining fish cooking juices to the sauce in the wok. Stir to mix well. Pour the spicy sauce over the fish.

Garnish with the coriander leaves and serve immediately with jasmine rice and Garlic or Ginger Pak Choy.

10 mins

10 mins

Thai Coconut Haddock 'Curry'

Serves 2

For the haddock marinade

250g (9oz) haddock loins, skinned, deboned and sliced to 2.5 x 5cm (1 x 2in) chunks

pinch of salt

pinch of ground white pepper

1 tsp Thai red curry paste

1 tbsp water

1 tbsp cornflour

For the curry

2 tbsp rapeseed oil

2 baby shallots, sliced, or 1 small red onion, diced

1 lemongrass, any tough outer leaf discarded, sliced into 5cm (2in) chunks

2 tbsp Thai red curry paste

1 tbsp cold water

200ml (7fl oz) coconut milk

100ml (3½fl oz) vegetable stock

100g (3½oz) sugar snap peas or mangetout

1 tbsp low-sodium light soy sauce or fish sauce

1 tbsp cornflour, blended with 2 tbsp cold water

To serve

fresh coriander or Thai basil leaves

1 red chilli, sliced (seeds in)

cooked jasmine rice (see page 22)

Haddock is a medium-flavoured fish and its loins are the meatiest and most expensive part but totally worth it for this dish. It is more like a chunky, brothy stew than a 'curry' – and it's totally delish and full of goodness. If you like a thicker sauce, add more cornflour slurry after seasoning.

Place the haddock pieces in a bowl with the salt, ground white pepper, Thai red curry paste and the measured water to loosen. Dust with the cornflour, then set aside to marinate.

Heat a wok over a medium heat until slightly smoking. Add 1 tablespoon of the rapeseed oil and give it a swirl. Add the shallots or red onion and lemongrass and stir-fry for a few seconds to release their aroma. Add the Thai red curry paste, stirring to distribute it around the wok. Add the other tablespoon of rapeseed oil and add the haddock pieces. Let them sear for a few seconds, then pour in the measured water around the edge to help create some steam and prevent the fish from sticking to the pan.

Add the coconut milk and the stock, then the sugar snap peas or mangetout and cook for 30 seconds to soften the veggies. Bring to the boil and cook for 4–5 minutes until the fish has turned opaque white.

Season with the light soy sauce or fish sauce, then add the cornflour slurry for a thicker consistency to the sauce. Garnish with the coriander or Thai basil and chilli and serve with jasmine rice.

15 mins

1 hour 20 mins (for a 1.8kg/4lb chicken)

Soy Butter Roast Chicken

Serves 4 to share

1 whole free range chicken
(approx. 1.8kg/4lb)

2–3 large pinches of sea salt

2–3 pinches of ground white pepper

3 small white onions, quartered

4 large garlic cloves, peeled and
slightly crushed but left whole

3 spring onions, trimmed and
sliced into 2.5cm (1in) pieces

150g (5½oz) melted butter

4–5 tbsp low-sodium
light soy sauce

1–2 tbsp rapeseed oil

**For the ginger spring onion
soy sauce**

7cm (3in) piece of fresh root
ginger, peeled and finely grated

1 red chilli, deseeded
and finely chopped

2 spring onions, trimmed
and finely sliced

3 tbsp low-sodium light soy sauce

2 tbsp mirin

1 tbsp toasted sesame oil

To serve

cooked jasmine rice (see page 22)

Easy Garlic or Ginger Pak Choy
(see page 180)

Once a month, my grandmother would slaughter a chicken; it was a prized time, a sacrifice we were grateful for. The whole animal was used: the neck and feet were used in a soup; half the carcass was steamed, the chicken shredded and eaten plain with some spring onion soy dressing; the other half was chopped up and cooked with the bones in a gingery oyster sauce stir-fry with mushrooms, which we ate with rice. This is the kind of sustainable eating that makes sense. With that ethos, this simple roast chicken is inspired by my grandmother – to make the soy butter roast chicken, brush the bird inside and out with melted 'butter' and soy, then roast until golden. The flavour is so delicious and rich in taste – perfect, simple cooking. Then you can turn the leftovers into Soy Butter Chicken Fried Lettuce with Hazelnuts (see page 118) and Soy Butter Chicken Spring Onion Chow Mein (see page 120). Enjoy!

Preheat the oven to 180°C (350°F), Gas Mark 4.

Place the chicken on a roasting rack and rub all over with the sea salt and ground white pepper to season. Stuff the chicken with the onions, garlic and spring onions.

Melt the butter in a small pan. Add the light soy sauce and mix well. Brush the soy butter all over the chicken, coating it well. Pour the remainder into the cavity. Drizzle the rapeseed oil all over the chicken.

Roast the chicken for 1 hour 20 minutes, turning the chicken around halfway through for even roasting. Use a cooking thermometer and pierce between the leg and thigh (the thickest part). The temperature should be greater than 78°C (172°F). Remove the chicken from the oven, then let it rest for 5 minutes.

While the chicken is resting, combine all the dressing ingredients in a large dressing bowl. To serve, carve the chicken at the dinner table, pass the dressing around and let people help themselves. Serve with plain jasmine rice and Garlic or Ginger Pak Choy.

Leftover Soy Butter Chicken Fried Lettuce with Hazelnuts

Serves 2

1 tbsp leftover chicken fat/juices or rapeseed oil

1cm (½in) slice of peeled fresh root ginger

½ red chilli, deseeded and sliced into thin matchsticks

100g (3½oz) offcuts from Soy Butter Roast Chicken (see page 114)

1 head of romaine lettuce, sliced lengthways on the diagonal into 5cm (2in) pieces

1 tbsp Shaohsing rice wine

1 tbsp low-sodium light soy sauce, with extra to serve

dash of toasted sesame oil

pinch of ground white pepper

1 spring onion, trimmed and sliced on the diagonal

1 handful of chopped toasted hazelnuts

To serve

cooked jasmine rice (see page 22)

dried chilli flakes

Shred the offcuts of the Soy Butter Roast Chicken (see page 116) and combine with some romaine lettuce in this quick and delicious stir-fry with toasted hazelnuts. You can fry in any chicken fat; the romaine lettuce wilts and is so sweet and tender cooked in this way.

Heat a wok over a high heat until slightly smoking. Add the chicken fat or rapeseed oil and give it a swirl. Add the ginger and chilli and stir-fry for a few seconds. Add the chicken pieces, followed by the romaine lettuce, and toss.

Season with the Shaohsing rice wine, light soy sauce, toasted sesame oil and ground white pepper and toss to mix well. Give it one last stir, then transfer to a serving dish. Sprinkle over the spring onion and chopped hazelnuts and serve immediately with jasmine rice. Serve with a dipping pot of light soy sauce and dried chilli flakes.

5 mins 5 mins

Leftover Soy Butter Chicken Spring Onion Chow Mein

Serves 2

1 tbsp leftover chicken fat/juices or rapeseed oil

1cm (½in) slice of peeled fresh root ginger

½ red chilli, deseeded and sliced into thin matchsticks

200g (7oz) offcuts from Soy Butter Roast Chicken (see page 114)

½ tsp chilli bean sauce

2 spring onions, trimmed and sliced on the angle

1 tbsp Shaohsing rice wine

200g (7oz) cooked egg noodles

1 large handful of beansprouts

1–2 tbsp low-sodium light soy sauce

dash of toasted sesame oil

pinch of ground white pepper

Sometimes spring onions add a fresh oniony bite to a dish, but I also love cooking them, especially in this dish, to release their sweet oniony flavour. Shred the offcuts of the Soy Butter Roast Chicken (see page 116) and combine with the spring onions and crunchy beansprouts in this quick and delicious chow mein using egg noodles. Add your favourite chilli sauce or chilli oil to kick some spice into the dish – umami and moreish. Enjoy!

Heat a wok over a high heat until slightly smoking. Add the leftover chicken fat or rapeseed oil and give it a swirl. Add the ginger and chilli and stir-fry for a few seconds. Add the chicken pieces, followed by the chilli bean sauce and spring onions, then toss.

Season with the Shaohsing rice wine. Add the cooked egg noodles and beansprouts and toss well. Season with the light soy sauce, toasted sesame oil and ground white pepper.

Give it one last stir, then transfer to a serving dish and serve immediately.

Roast Chicken & Mushroom Puffs

Makes 6 puffs • Serves 2

For the marinade

4 boneless, skinless chicken thighs, diced

3 garlic cloves, finely chopped

5cm (2in) piece pf fresh root ginger, peeled and finely grated

2 tbsp oyster sauce

For the stir-fry

6–8 dried shiitake mushrooms

1 tbsp rapeseed oil

1 tsp dark soy sauce

1 tbsp Shaohsing rice wine or dry sherry

1 tbsp low-sodium light soy sauce

dash of toasted sesame oil

pinch of dried coriander

For the pastry

225g (8oz) ready-made rolled puff pastry

beaten egg, to glaze

white sesame seeds, for sprinkling

This is inspired by the Cantonese roast pork pastry puffs you get at dim sum restaurants. I love the flavours of oyster sauce, chicken and mushrooms so this is my version. Oyster sauce pairs so well with chicken and mushrooms, and this flavour is perfect in a puff. Easy and delicious, great comfort food – this one will be love at first bite.

Combine all the ingredients for the marinade in a large dish, ensuring the chicken is well coated. Cover and leave in the refrigerator to marinate for 1 hour.

Place the shiitake mushrooms in a bowl of hot water for 20 minutes to rehydrate, then drain and finely dice. Set aside in the refrigerator.

Heat a wok or pan over a medium heat. Add the rapeseed oil and give it a swirl. Add the mushrooms and stir-fry for 1 minute. Add the marinated chicken pieces, let them sear and brown for 15 seconds and then stir-fry for 2 minutes. Season with the dark soy sauce and toss well together. Season with the Shaohsing rice wine or sherry and toss again. Season with the light soy sauce, then toss well once more. Add the toasted sesame oil, stir, and sprinkle over the dried coriander. Tip out on a plate and leave to cool at room temperature for 20 minutes. Then cover and refrigerate.

Preheat the oven to 180°C (350°F), Gas Mark 4. Line a roasting tray with baking paper.

Unroll the puff pastry and cut into 12 triangles, measuring 5cm (2in) on each side. Place a teaspoon of the chilled chicken filling in the middle of one triangle, then place another piece on top. Press the edges down to seal and then fold over to give slightly rounded edges. Brush the beaten egg over the top, place on the lined roasting tray and sprinkle sesame seeds over the top of the parcel. Repeat until you have 6 parcels, then bake them in the oven for 20 minutes until the pastry is golden. Serve immediately.

Sweet & Sour Chicken

Serves 2 or 4 to share

For the marinade

½ tsp Chinese five spice

pinch of ground white pepper

1 tbsp Shaohsing rice wine

1 tbsp low-sodium light soy sauce

For the chicken

400g (14oz) chicken thighs, cut into 2.5cm (1in) cubes

1 tbsp rapeseed oil

1 garlic clove, finely chopped

2.5cm (1in) piece of fresh root ginger, peeled and finely grated

1 white onion, cut into 2.5cm (1in) chunks

1 red chilli, deseeded and finely chopped

1 tbsp Shaohsing rice wine

1 red pepper, cored, deseeded and cut into 2.5cm (1in) chunks

1 yellow pepper, cored, deseeded and cut into 2.5cm (1in) chunks

1 small handful of fresh or canned pineapple, drained and juice retained

dash of toasted sesame oil

pinch of ground white pepper

1–2 spring onions, trimmed and finely chopped, to garnish

For the sweet and sour sauce

100ml (3½fl oz) cold vegetable stock

50ml (2fl oz) canned pineapple juice (see above)

1 tbsp low-sodium light soy sauce

1 tbsp ketchup

2 tbsp clear rice vinegar

2 tbsp golden syrup

1 tbsp cornflour

This is my ultimate sweet and sour chicken. The list of ingredients may seem long but I promise this one is well worth the effort. The layers of flavours in this dish are simply divine. Using fresh pineapple would make it a treat but canned pineapple works perfectly too; it's just up to you.

In a bowl, mix together the marinade ingredients with the chicken. Leave to marinate for 10–15 minutes.

In a jug, add all the ingredients for the sweet and sour sauce and stir well.

Heat a wok over a high heat until smoking. Add the rapeseed oil and give it a swirl. Add the garlic, ginger, onion and red chilli. Stir-fry for 5–10 seconds, until the onion starts to caramelize. Add the chicken pieces and let them sear on one side for 5–10 seconds before you flip them to cook on the underside. Add the Shaohsing rice wine and cook, stirring, for 3–4 minutes until the chicken is cooked through.

Add the peppers and toss for 15 seconds until softened. Add the pineapple. Add the sweet and sour sauce and bring to the boil. Cook for 20 seconds until the sauce has reduced and coats the chicken and vegetables.

Season with the toasted sesame oil and ground white pepper and sprinkle over the spring onions, then serve immediately.

10 mins

10 mins

Chinese Chicken Curry

Serves 2

200g (7oz) skin-off chicken thighs, cut into 2.5cm (1in) chunks

pinch of sea salt flakes

pinch of ground white pepper

1 tbsp cornflour

1 tbsp rapeseed oil

1 garlic clove, finely chopped

2.5cm (1in) piece of fresh root ginger, peeled and finely grated

1 green chilli, deseeded and finely chopped

½ white onion, sliced

1 tbsp Shaohsing rice wine or dry sherry

1 tsp dark soy sauce

1 small carrot, trimmed and sliced diagonally into ovals

1 handful of broccoli florets

1 spring onion, trimmed and sliced into 2cm (¾in) pieces on the diagonal to garnish

For the curry sauce

150ml (5fl oz) cold fresh chicken stock

1 star anise

1 tsp ground turmeric

½ tsp Madras hot curry powder

1 tsp light brown sugar

1 tbsp cornflour

This Chinese chicken curry is similar to what you would get from a Chinese takeaway. Mildly spicy and sweet, it's a warm and comforting dish, perfect for winter and delicious with jasmine rice.

Place the chicken in a bowl, season with the salt and white pepper and dust with the cornflour. Mix well to coat, then set aside.

Whisk together all the ingredients for the curry sauce in a jug, then set aside.

Heat a wok over a high heat until smoking. Add the rapeseed oil and give it a swirl. Add the garlic, ginger, chilli and sliced onion and stir-fry for a few seconds to release their aroma.

Add the chicken and let it sit for 10 seconds to sear and brown, then flip it over. Add the Shaohsing rice wine or dry sherry and toss the chicken for 2 minutes until cooked through.

Add the carrot and broccoli and toss for 1 minute, then drizzle a tablespoon of cold water around the edge of the wok to create steam to help cook the vegetables.

Pour in the sauce and bring to the boil. Cook for 10 seconds to thicken up. Transfer to a serving plate, garnish with the spring onion and serve immediately.

10 mins · 30 mins

Mouth-watering Chicken

Serves 2 or 4 to share

For the chicken

1 bunch of spring onions, trimmed and sliced into 2.5cm (1in) pieces

4 skin-on chicken thighs

2.5cm (1in) piece of fresh root ginger, peeled and finely grated

2 tbsp Shaohsing rice wine

½ tsp ground Sichuan pepper

¼ tsp ground sea salt

½ tsp crushed dried chilli flakes

1 litre (1¾ pints) water

For the hot dressing

2 tbsp vegetable oil

½ tsp ground Sichuan pepper

½ tsp crushed dried chilli flakes

1 tbsp low-sodium light soy sauce

1 tbsp rice vinegar

1 tbsp toasted sesame oil

To garnish

toasted sesame seeds

fresh coriander

To serve

Smacked Garlic Cucumber Salad (see page 183)

cooked jasmine rice (see page 22)

chilli bean sauce

Vegan Option
Use blanched sliced oyster mushrooms instead of the chicken.

Kou shui jī **is a classic Sichuan dish. Traditionally a whole chicken is boiled with ginger, spring onions, Chinese leeks and rice wine. My Sichuan-style version of** *kou shui jī* **is so easy to cook and not as spicy as the original. Chicken thighs are coated well with grated ginger, rice wine, salt, Sichuan pepper and dried chilli flakes, then steamed (instead of boiled) until tender. Mouth-wateringly delicious!**

Reserve 2 of the spring onions for garnish, then place the remaining pieces on a shallow heatproof dish. Lay the chicken thighs on the spring onions. Rub the chicken with the grated ginger, season with the Shaohsing rice wine, ground Sichuan pepper, ground sea salt and chilli flakes and mix well, ensuring the chicken is well coated in the seasoning.

Fill a wok or pan with the measured water, place a stainless-steel steamer rack over the top, then place the heatproof dish with the chicken on top of the rack. Cover, bring to the boil and steam over a medium heat for 25 minutes.

To check if the chicken is cooked, put a skewer through the chunkiest part of the thigh: it should go through without resistance. When it's done, take it off the heat. The chicken will be piping hot, so carefully shred the meat off the bone with a knife and fork. Slice and shred the skin into bite-size pieces, too. Reserve the cooking juices. Set all this aside.

Heat a small wok or pan over a medium heat. Add the oil.

In a small heatproof bowl add the ground Sichuan pepper and chilli flakes. Pour the hot oil over the spices; they should sizzle. Then add the light soy sauce, rice vinegar, toasted sesame oil and 4 tablespoons of the reserved cooking juices and mix well. Spoon this sauce over the chicken.

Garnish with a small sprinkling of toasted sesame seeds, spring onion and coriander. Serve the chicken with the Smacked Garlic Cucumber Salad, jasmine rice and a dollop of chilli bean sauce on the side.

5 mins
10 mins

Next Day Rainbow Chicken Bone Broth with Shiitake Mushroom Noodles

Serves 2

1 litre (1¾ pints) chicken stock

4 leftover chicken thigh bones, plus some strips of meat (see page 126 or page 128)

2.5cm (1in) piece of fresh root ginger, peeled and sliced

1 tbsp Shaohsing rice wine

200g (7oz) fresh shiitake mushrooms, stalks removed and caps whole

1 handful of prepared stir-fry rainbow vegetables

1 tbsp low-sodium light soy sauce

1 tsp toasted sesame oil

1–2 pinches of ground white pepper

150g (5½oz) cooked rice noodles

1–2 spring onions, trimmed and finely sliced

This warming noodle soup is made using leftover chicken thigh bones from page 126 or page 128. Just add fresh whole shiitake mushrooms, rainbow vegetables and cooked rice noodles and you have a quick, warming and nutritious bowl.

Heat the chicken stock in a pan over a high heat. Add the chicken bones, then the ginger. Pour in the Shaohsing rice wine, bring to the boil, then let it simmer for 5–10 minutes.

Add the shiitake mushrooms and mixed stir-fry vegetables, then season with the light soy sauce, toasted sesame oil and ground white pepper.

Boil the kettle, then pour the hot water over the cooked rice noodles to refresh them. Drain well and tip into 2 bowls.

Ladle over the hot stock (discarding the bones), add the mushrooms and vegetables, then sprinkle over the spring onions and serve immediately.

10 mins 15 mins

Roast Chilli Chicken

Serves 2

4 bone-in, skin-on chicken thighs

2 pinches of sea salt

2 pinches of ground white pepper

2 pinches of Chinese five
spice powder

1 tbsp chilli bean sauce

2 tbsp rapeseed oil

1 tsp cornflour

2 tbsp Shaohsing rice wine

1 tbsp low-sodium light soy sauce

For the veggies

200g (7oz) long-stem broccoli,
sliced into 2.5 (1in) pieces

2 spring onions, trimmed and
sliced into 2.5cm (1in) pieces

1 tbsp rapeseed oil

1 tbsp low-sodium light soy sauce

handful of cashew nuts

For the chicken

1 tsp golden syrup

pinch of dried chilli flakes

To serve

1 lime, sliced in half

cooked jasmine rice (see page 22)

Vegan Option
Use oyster mushrooms
instead of the chicken
and cook them for less
than half the time

This is a more-ish spiced chicken dish that is super delicious. You could roast the chicken in a preheated oven at 180°C (350°F), Gas Mark 4 degrees for 30–40 minutes or cook it in a wok or pan as below. The Chinese five spice imparts the flavours of fennel, cinnamon, Sichuan pepper, cloves and star anise, making this dish super moreish. The chilli bean sauce gives a hint of umami spice. The chicken is served with some spring onion and cashew nuts and brushed with golden syrup for a touch of sweetness. Save the extra chicken thighs and bones for Chicken Bone Broth (see page 127) the next day to make this a perfect two-for-one dinner.

Place the chicken thighs in a bowl, season with the salt, ground white pepper, Chinese five spice and the chilli bean sauce. Rub the seasoning all over the chicken well and let it marinate for 5–10 minutes.

Heat a wok or pan to a medium–high heat. Add the rapeseed oil and give it a swirl. Dust the chicken pieces with the cornflour and, using tongs, lift into the wok or pan, skin-side down. Let it cook for 15 seconds, to settle and brown, then flip to the other side. Reduce the heat to medium and cook and sizzle for 10–12 minutes.

Season with the Shaohsing rice wine, then cook for another 1 minute, checking the chicken is cooked through. Finally season with the light soy sauce, then remove from the pan and set aside.

Add the broccoli and spring onion to the wok with the rapeseed oil, season with light soy sauce, then toss in the cashew nuts. Cook in the chicken juices and oil for 1–2 minutes until the veggies are tender and the nuts are toasted.

Brush the golden syrup over the chicken and sprinkle over the dried chilli flakes.

Serve 2 chicken thighs alongside the broccoli, spring onions and cashew nuts, with the lime halves and jasmine rice on the side. Carve the remaining 2 chicken thighs, reserving the bones, and store in an airtight container in the refrigerator for Next Day Rainbow Chicken Bone Broth with Shiitake Mushroom Noodles.

Wok For Less

5 mins 5 mins

Roast Chicken Fried Rice

Serves 2

1 tbsp rapeseed oil

70g (2½oz) frozen peas

1 Chinese leaf, finely sliced

1 tbsp Shaohsing rice wine

200g (7oz) cooked jasmine rice
(see page 22)

100g (3½oz) Roast Chilli Chicken
(see page 126), shredded into
1cm (½in) strips

pinch of Chinese five spice

1 tsp dark soy sauce

1–2 tbsp low-sodium light soy sauce

1 tbsp toasted sesame oil

pinch of ground white pepper

1 spring onion, trimmed and finely
sliced on the angle, to garnish

chilli bean sauce, to serve

For this you'll need 2 thighs leftover from the Roast Chilli Chicken recipe (see page 128), along with some wok-fried Chinese leaf and leftover cooked jasmine rice. Chicken thigh is really the best meat for this quick and easy supper.

Heat a wok over a high heat until smoking. Add the rapeseed oil and give it a swirl. Add the frozen peas and Chinese leaf and stir-fry for less than a minute. Add the Shaohsing rice wine and cook for 1–2 minutes.

Add the cooked jasmine rice and, using a wooden spoon or metal spatula, start to gently break apart the rice grains: not in a stabbing motion but just tossing the ingredients well for 1–2 minutes.

Add the chilli chicken strips and toss together for 1 minute. Season with the Chinese five spice, dark soy sauce, light soy sauce, toasted sesame oil and ground white pepper. Toss well.

Garnish with the spring onion and serve immediately with chilli bean sauce on the side.

15 mins   25 mins

Easy Hainan Chicken Rice

Serves 4

For the rice

300g (10½oz) jasmine rice,
rinsed until the water runs clear
(see page 22)

500ml (18fl oz) water

For the poaching liquid

1 litre (1¾ pints) water

4 boneless, skinless chicken thighs

2.5cm (1in) piece of fresh root
ginger, peeled and sliced

2 star anise

1 tbsp Shaohsing rice wine

3 spring onions, trimmed and
sliced into 2.5cm (1in) pieces

large pinch of sea salt

½ tsp whole white peppercorns

½ tsp Sichuan peppercorns

To serve

raw green chilli, ginger and spring
onion salsa verde (see page 191)

½ cucumber, peeled with a potato
peeler into long, thin slices

low-sodium light soy sauce

dark soy sauce

black rice vinegar

chilli bean sauce

This dish is inspired by the Chinese island of Hainan. Hainan chicken rice, a southern Chinese classic, is served all over Asia and is the national dish of Singapore. Those who love Hainan chicken rice know you enjoy it with your favourite condiment – light or dark soy sauce, black rice vinegar, raw chilli sauce... it's up to you, but whichever you choose, serve with a bowl of the chicken broth for extra goodness.

Place the washed rice in a medium pan. Fill with the measured water. Bring to boil, then turn the heat to low, put the lid on and gently simmer for 20 minutes until the grains are cooked. Fluff with a fork.

Meanwhile to make the poaching liquid, in a wok or medium pan add the measured water, chicken thighs, ginger, star anise, Shaohsing wine, spring onions, salt, whole white peppercorns and Sichuan peppercorns. Bring to a gentle simmer and cook for 15–20 minutes, until the chicken is white and cooked through. Remove from the heat and keep the chicken warm in the liquid until ready to serve.

Remove the chicken from the pan, drain, reserving the broth and discarding the aromatics, and shred on a board.

To assemble, portion the rice on 4 plates. Place the chicken on the side and dress with the salsa verde over the top.

Serve with the cucumber slices, separate pots of light soy sauce, dark soy sauce, black rice vinegar and chilli bean sauce, and a bowl of the hot broth to moisten the rice.

Carve the remaining 2 chicken thighs, reserving the bones, and store in an airtight container in the refrigerator for Next Day Rainbow Chicken Bone Broth.

5 mins

45–50 mins

Roast Hoisin Chicken Wings

Serves 2

400g (14oz) chicken wings

225g (8oz) jar of shop-bought hoisin sauce

black sesame seeds, to garnish

Egg Fried Rice (see page 30) or a salad from the salads & sides chapter (see page 176)

This delicious roast supper is ever so easy to make. The hoisin sauce tastes sweet and savoury, which makes it perfect in dishes served with salad or a simple egg fried rice.

Preheat the oven to 180°C (350°F), Gas Mark 4.

Place the chicken wings in a large roasting tray. Pour over the jar of hoisin sauce to smother the chicken wings, ensuring they are completely covered. Roast in the oven for 45–50 minutes.

Remove and serve, garnished with toasted sesame seeds, with Egg Fried Rice or salad.

Vegan Option Use assorted mushrooms instead of the chicken wings and roast for 20 minutes

Hoisin Roast Duck Legs

Serves 2–4 to share

6 skin-on duck legs

For the marinade

2 garlic cloves, minced

5cm (2in) piece of fresh root ginger, peeled and finely grated

2 tbsp Shaohsing rice wine

1 tsp Chinese five spice powder

3 tbsp golden syrup

3 tbsp hoisin sauce

1 tbsp chilli bean sauce

1 tbsp dark soy sauce

pinch of sea salt

To serve

cooked jasmine rice (see page 22)

Smacked Garlic Cucumber Salad (see page 183)

Radish, Cucumber & Cherry Tomato Quick 'Pickle' (see page 183)

This recipe is super easy – marinate the duck legs with Chinese seasonings and roast in a hot oven. Serve with Smacked Garlic Cucumber Salad and my punchy Radish Pickle with jasmine rice. It makes a brilliant easy dinner.

Place the duck legs in a resealable bag, then add all the marinade ingredients and shake to distribute evenly. Marinate in the refrigerator for at least 1 hour.

Preheat the oven to 180°C (350°F), Gas Mark 4. Line a roasting tray with baking paper.

Place the duck legs (including any marinade left in the bag) round-side up on the lined roasting tray. Roast for 40 minutes, then turn heat up to 220°C (425°F), Gas Mark 7 and cook the duck legs for a further 10 minutes for medium–well done.

Remove and set the duck aside to rest for 5 minutes. Serve 4 of the legs (keeping 2 legs and bones for subsequent leftover recipes) with jasmine rice, Smacked Garlic Cucumber Salad and Radish, Cucumber & Cherry Tomato Quick 'Pickle'.

Shred the remaining 2 duck legs, reserving the bones, and store in an airtight container in the refrigerator for another meal – Roast Duck x Spring Onion Fried Rice (see page 139) or Roast Duck Noodles (see page 138).

 Vegan Option Use assorted mushrooms instead of the chicken wings and roast for 20 minutes

Hoisin Roast Duck Noodles

Serves 2

800ml (1½ pints) chicken stock

4–6 leftover duck bones, plus some shredded meat from the Hoisin Roasted Duck Legs (see page 134)

2.5cm (1in) piece of fresh root ginger, peeled and sliced

1 tbsp Shaohsing rice wine

2 heads of pak choy, sliced into quarters

1 tbsp light soy sauce

1 tsp toasted sesame oil

1–2 pinches of ground white pepper

250g (9oz) cooked egg noodles

1–2 spring onions, trimmed and finely sliced

½ red chilli, deseeded and finely sliced on the angle

I love this super speedy supper in minutes. It is perfect for using the Hoisin Roast Duck Legs on page 136. The broth is delicious with warming ginger and is super simple and comforting. Use whatever veggies you might have in the fridge. Enjoy!

Heat the chicken stock in a wok over a high heat. Add the duck bones and the sliced ginger. Pour in the Shaohsing rice wine, bring to the boil and let it simmer for 5–10 minutes.

Add the pak choy quarters and cook for 1 minute. Season with the light soy sauce, toasted sesame oil and ground white pepper.

Boil the kettle, then pour the hot water over the cooked egg noodles to refresh them. Drain well and tip into 2 bowls.

Top with shredded duck meat and ladle over the hot stock (discarding the bones). Sprinkle over the sliced spring onions and red chilli and serve immediately with the pak choy on the side.

Vegan Option Use smoked tofu strips instead of the roast duck, vegetable stock instead of chicken and rice noodles instead of egg noodles

5 mins   5 mins

Roast Duck x Spring Onion Fried Rice

Serves 2

1 tbsp rapeseed oil

2 spring onions, trimmed and cut into 1cm (½in) slices, white and green parts separated

leftover shredded meat from 2 Hoisin Roasted Duck Legs (see page 134)

pinch of Chinese five spice powder

½ tsp dark soy sauce

300g (10½oz) cooked jasmine rice (see page 22)

1–2 tbsp low-sodium light soy sauce

dash of toasted sesame oil

pinch of ground white pepper

To garnish

1 handful of roasted, unsalted cashew nuts

1 red chilli, deseeded and finely chopped

This is a great one if you have leftover shredded duck legs (see page 136). The five spice imparts warming notes, the spring onions add bite, and the cashew nuts have a lovely moreish crunch. Enjoy!

Heat a wok over a medium heat until smoking. Add the rapeseed oil and give it a swirl. Add the white parts of the spring onion, then toss for less than 10 seconds. Add the roast duck meat and toss for 10 seconds. Add the Chinese five spice powder, then season with the dark soy sauce.

Add the cooked jasmine rice and, using a wooden spoon or metal spatula, start to gently break apart the rice grains: not in a stabbing motion but just tossing the ingredients well for 1–2 minutes.

Drizzle over the light soy sauce and then quickly toss to coat the grains well and evenly colour the rice. Sprinkle over the remaining green parts of the spring onions. Season with the toasted sesame oil and ground white pepper. Sprinkle over the cashew nuts and red chilli. Serve immediately.

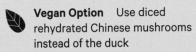

Vegan Option Use diced rehydrated Chinese mushrooms instead of the duck

10 mins 2 mins

Hoisin Roast Duck Lettuce Cups

Makes about 12–15 lettuce cups • Serves 2

leftover shredded meat from
2 Hoisin Roasted Duck Legs
(*see* page 134)

2 heads of Gem lettuce, leaves
separated

10 small radishes, thinly sliced

2 spring onions, trimmed and
sliced into very thin long strips
and soaked in ice water for
5 minutes to curl up, then drained

3 tbsp hoisin sauce, to serve

This dish is a great alternative idea for the Hoisin Roast Duck Legs on page 136 by serving them in super refreshing, tasty and healthy 'lettuce cups'.

This dish can be served at room temperature, but if you'd like to reheat the duck, dry toss it in a small pan over a medium heat for 2 minutes.

Place the Gem lettuce leaves, cucumber slices and spring onion curls in small serving dishes. Pour the hoisin sauce into dipping bowls with small serving spoons.

Serve at the table so your guests can assemble themselves: place some shredded duck on a lettuce cup, garnish with a slice of radish and spring onion curl, and finally spoon on the hoisin sauce (to taste). Or you can portion each lettuce cup as ready-to-eat canapés.

5 mins

45–50 mins

Char Siu Pork Ribs with Egg Fried Rice

Serves 2

500g (1lb 2oz) baby pork ribs

225g (8oz) jar of shop-bought char siu sauce

toasted white sesame seeds, to garnish

Egg Fried Rice (see page 30) or a salad from the salads & sides chapters (see page 176), to serve

'Char siu' in Cantonese means 'fork roasted'. There's nothing more delicious than roasted char siu pork belly or ribs – this recipe works for either cut of meat. Seek out a good-quality char siu sauce that pairs really well with pork. This recipe is great to cook in the oven or on the barbecue in the summer. Delicious served with salad, fried rice or fried noodles.

Preheat the oven to 180°C (350°F), Gas Mark 4.

Place the pork ribs in a large roasting tray. Pour over the jar of char siu sauce, coating the ribs well to ensure they are totally covered.

Roast in the oven for 45–50 minutes.

Remove from the oven, garnish with the sesame seeds and serve with the Egg Fried Rice or salad.

Char Siu Pork Spring Onion Noodles

Serves 2

800ml (1½ pints) chicken stock

2.5cm (1in) piece of fresh root ginger, peeled and sliced

1 tbsp Shaohsing rice wine

2 heads of pak choy, sliced into quarters

1 tbsp low-sodium light soy sauce

1 tsp toasted sesame oil

1–2 pinches of ground white pepper

250g (9oz) cooked egg noodles

220g (7¾oz) Char Sui Roast from page 145, cut into 1cm- (½in)-thick slices

To serve

1–2 spring onions, trimmed and finely sliced

½ red chilli, deseeded and finely sliced on the diagonal

This recipe uses leftover Char Sui Roast slices from page 145, served on top of a delicious egg noodle base for a quick, moreish supper.

Heat the chicken stock in a wok over a high heat. Add the ginger, then pour in the Shaohsing rice wine, bring to the boil, then let it simmer for 5–10 minutes.

Add the pak choy and cook for 1 minute, then season with the light soy sauce, toasted sesame oil and ground white pepper.

Boil the kettle and pour the hot water over the cooked egg noodles to refresh them. Drain well and tip into 2 bowls.

Ladle over the hot stock. Top with sliced char siu pork and pak choy. Sprinkle over the spring onion and red chilli and serve immediately.

5 mins + 2 hrs marinating

45 mins

Sticky Char Siu Roast Pork Crispy Noodles with Hot and Sour Soy Sauce

Serves 2 or 4 to share

1 × 500g (1lb 2oz) pork fillet

For the char siu roast pork marinade

2 garlic cloves, crushed and finely chopped

5cm (2in) piece of fresh root ginger, peeled and finely grated

50ml (2fl oz) low-sodium light soy sauce

50ml (2fl oz) Shaohsing rice wine

3 tbsp golden syrup

1 tbsp hoisin sauce

2 tbsp miso sauce

1 tbsp rapeseed oil

pinch of sea salt

pinch of ground white pepper

For the noodles

300g (10½oz) dried noodles, or 300g (10½oz) cooked egg noodles

1 tbsp toasted sesame oil

6 tbsp rapeseed oil

100g (3½oz) baby pak choy, separated and blanched

For the hot and sour soy sauce

4 tbsp low-sodium light soy sauce

5g (⅛oz) fresh coriander, finely chopped

3 garlic cloves, finely chopped

1 tbsp chilli oil

1 tbsp clear rice vinegar

1 tbsp soft brown sugar

The combination of hot and sour sauce, char siu roast pork and crispy noodles makes this dish a winner. You can make your own char siu roast pork or buy it from a good Chinese restaurant. The best bit about making your own is that you can make as much as you want, so you can have leftovers for roast pork sandwiches. My char siu sauce recipe is below or you could buy it ready-made if you don't have the time.

To make the char siu roast pork, cut slashes into the sides of the pork fillet. Combine all the marinade ingredients in a large bowl, then add the pork and marinate for a couple of hours.

Preheat the oven to 200°C (400°F), Gas Mark 6. Remove the pork and place it on a rack set over a roasting tray, pouring over the marinade. Roast the pork for 20 minutes, then turn the fillet over and brush with the cooking juices from the tray, basting well. Reduce the temperature to 180°C (350°F), Gas Mark 4 and roast for a further 20 minutes. Remove and let it rest.

Meanwhile, prepare the noodles. If using dried noodles, bring a pan of water to the boil. Add the noodles and cook for 3 minutes. Drain, refresh under cold water, then drain again. Add the toasted sesame oil and toss well. If using cooked noodles, add to the wok.

Heat a wok over a high heat and add the rapeseed oil. Transfer the nest of noodles to the pan and shallow fry them until crispy, cooking for 2 minutes on each side. Place the crispy nest of noodles on a serving plate.

To prepare the char siu roast pork, cut half of it into 0.5cm (¼ in) thick slices, saving the remaining half for sandwiches. In a small bowl, mix together the sauce ingredients.

Place the wok over a medium heat, then add the roast pork and the hot and sour soy sauce. Stir-fry for 1 minute until the sauce begins to caramelize. Add the baby pak choy and stir-fry for 30 seconds.

Remove from the heat and top the noodles with the char siu roast pork and baby pak choy mixture along with any remaining sauce. Serve immediately.

10 mins + 10 mins marinating

4 mins

Grilled Char Siu Pork Brioche Burger

Makes 2 burgers

For the grilled char siu pork

1 garlic clove, finely chopped

2 tbsp char siu sauce

1 tbsp Shaohsing rice wine

220g (7¾oz) pork loin, cut into 1cm- (½in)-thick slices

1 tbsp rapeseed oil

For the buns

2 brioche buns, halved

2 tsp hoisin sauce

Sesame Slaw (see page 182)

2 tbsp spicy mayonnaise

1 tsp chilli bean sauce

To serve

Gem lettuce leaves

a few rings of red onion

a few beef tomato slices

hoisin sauce

This is inspired by the sweet and savoury flavours of Chinese cooking. Grilled char siu pork loins are topped with a Chinese coleslaw for an East-meets-West feast. Serve with salad on the side and a pot of hoisin sauce for dipping.

Mix together the garlic, char siu sauce and Shaohsing rice wine in a large bowl. Mix in the thin pork loin pieces and leave to marinate for 10 minutes.

Remove the pork from the marinade and rub on all sides with the rapeseed oil.

Heat a griddle pan over a high heat. Place the pork loins on the grill and cook for 1½ minutes on each side. Set aside to rest.

Slather a layer of hoisin sauce on the lid and base of each brioche bun. Place the buns on the griddle pan for 20 seconds to warm up and then remove.

Place a piece of pork loin on the base of each brioche, then top with slaw. Drizzle over some spicy mayonnaise and chilli bean sauce. Serve immediately with some Gem lettuce, red onion and tomatoes on the side and a pot of hoisin sauce for dipping.

10 mins 1 hrs

Chilli Bean Beef Pasta

Serves 2 or 4 to share

600g (1lb 5oz) beef shin

2 pinches of salt

2 pinches of ground black pepper

2 tbsp rapeseed oil

1 large white onion, finely diced

3 garlic cloves, finely chopped

2.5cm (1in) piece of fresh root ginger, peeled

2 celery sticks, cut into 0.5cm (¼in) slices

2 carrots, trimmed and cut into 0.5cm (¼in) dice

1 tbsp chilli bean sauce

1 tbsp low-sodium light soy sauce

1 tsp dark soy sauce

1 tbsp oyster sauce

1 tbsp Shaohsing rice wine or dry sherry

1 litre (1¾ pints) beef stock or vegetable stock

1 bay leaf

1 star anise

300g (10½oz) cooked wide noodles, egg noodles or tagliatelle pasta

To garnish

fresh coriander, leaves picked and stems finely diced

1 red chilli, sliced on the deep angle

This is a delicious Chinese–Italian fusion pasta dish with tonnes of umami. The sweetness of the oyster sauce and the rich, beany, salty notes of soy sauce really make this dish a winner. It makes a super satisfying meal when served with egg noodles or fresh tagliatelle pasta, and add a hunk of your favourite bread and glass of red wine for the ultimate treat.

Season the beef shin with the salt and ground black pepper.

Heat a wok or pan over a high heat. Add 1 tablespoon of the rapeseed oil and give it a swirl. Add the beef shin and sear and brown it for 6–7 minutes all over. Remove from the wok and set the beef aside.

Reduce the heat to medium and add the remaining tablespoon of rapeseed oil. Add the onions and fry for 5–10 minutes until translucent. Add the garlic, ginger, celery and carrots and cook for 3 minutes.

Add the chilli bean sauce, then season with the light soy, dark soy and oyster sauces and Shaohsing rice wine or dry sherry. Add the stock, bay leaf and star anise. Add the beef back to the wok or pan, then put the lid on and cook over a medium–low heat for 1½ hours.

Remove the meat and slice it up.

Increase the heat to high and boil the sauce for about 15 minutes until reduced and thickened.

Bring a pot of water to the boil. Add the noodles or fresh pasta and cook according to the packet instructions. Drain, then transfer the pasta to the wok or pan and stir everything together well.

Portion into individual bowls and top with coriander stems, coriander leaves and the red chilli.

15 mins

3 hrs
40 mins
– 4 hrs 10
mins

Chilli Beef Brisket

Serves 2 or 4 to share

3 tbsp rapeseed oil

1kg (2lb 4oz) rolled boneless beef brisket

8–10 garlic cloves

1 large carrot, trimmed and sliced into rounds

4 celery sticks, sliced into 2.5cm (1in) pieces

1 star anise

3 dried chillies

1 tsp Sichuan peppercorns (optional)

1 tbsp chilli bean paste

2 litres (3½ pints) vegetable, beef or chicken stock

500ml (18fl oz) water

To serve

red chilli, ginger and spring onion soy salsa verde (see page 191)

cooked jasmine rice (see page 22), roast potatoes or cooked egg noodles

steamed vegetables

This Chinese Chilli Beef Brisket is a total crowd pleaser. You could opt to cook the brisket low and slow in the oven like I have, or in a slow cooker or in a wok on medium–low heat with the lid on; they all work. The oven is the easiest and most fuss free. Any which way, the beef is perfect stuffed in shop-bought bao buns (see page 152) or served with roasted potatoes and steamed veggies of your choice. The salsa verde makes a super punchy and delicious sauce.

Preheat the oven to 150°C (300°F), Gas Mark 2.

Heat a deep, cast iron casserole dish over a high heat, then add the rapeseed oil. Add the brisket and brown for 7–8 minutes on all sides. Add the garlic, sliced carrot, sliced celery, star anise, dried chillies, Sichuan pepper corns, if using, chilli bean paste, stock and measured water. Cover with a lid. Place in the oven and cook for 3½–4 hours.

Remove the brisket from the oven, place the brisket on a board, then slice. Serve with rice, roast potatoes or cooked egg noodles, steamed vegetables and the salsa verde.

Vegan Option You can use vegetablesand chunky tofu instead of the beef; just halve the cooking time for a delicious stew

Wok For Less

10 mins   5 mins

Chilli Beef Brisket Noodles

Serves 2

500ml (18fl oz) chicken stock

2.5cm (1in) piece of fresh root ginger, peeled and sliced into coins

2 heads of pak choy, sliced into quarters

250g (9oz) cooked egg noodles

2–3 chunky slices, about 150g (5½oz), Chilli Beef Brisket (see page 146), plus juices, reheated

1 spring onion, trimmed and finely sliced

½ red chilli, deseeded and finely sliced on the diagonal

This is the perfect way to use up leftover brisket, by making a delicious, simple hot noodle soup. Frankly, you can use whatever ingredients you have – any greens if you don't have pak choy, or mushrooms, peppers or any odds and ends – for a warming nourishing bowl.

In a medium pan or wok, heat the chicken stock over a high heat. Add the ginger coins and the pak choy quarters and bring to a gentle simmer.

Boil the kettle and pour the hot water over the cooked egg noodles to refresh them, then drain well and pour into 2 bowls.

Top each bowl with leftover heated brisket and pour over some juices. Ladle the hot stock over both bowls, sprinkle over the spring onion and red chilli and serve the pak choy on the side.

Vegan Option Use veggie stock, rice noodles and smoked tofu strips

10 mins 5 mins

Chilli Beef Brisket Baos

Serves 2 or 4 to share

4–8 frozen bao buns

400g (14oz) leftover Chilli Beef Brisket (see page 148)

a few dollops of hoisin sauce

½ cucumber, sliced into strips

2 spring onions, trimmed and sliced into julienne strips

Pair leftover Chilli Beef Brisket with frozen shop-bought baos and crunchy veggies like cucumber and spring onions. Top with any leftover Salsa Verde (see page 191) or drizzle over hoisin sauce and eat immediately.

Line a bamboo steamer with baking paper, then place the bao buns in. Place the bamboo steamer over a wok half-filled with water. Bring the water to the boil and steam for 5 minutes over a high heat until the buns are soft. Remove from the heat and leave in the steamer to keep hot.

Warm the leftover brisket in a wok or pan over a medium heat for 3–4 minutes.

Spoon the hoisin sauce into a sauce bowl, then place the buns, warmed brisket, cucumber and spring onions on the table and serve immediately.

5 mins

12 mins

Soy Butter Lamb Chops

Serves 4 to share

8 lamb chops, on the bone

2–3 pinches of sea salt

2–3 pinches of ground black pepper

2 tbsp rapeseed oil or olive oil

2–3 garlic cloves, crushed

2 spring onions, trimmed and sliced into 5cm (2in) pieces

2 cubes (30g/1oz) of butter

1 tbsp low-sodium light soy sauce

Basic Egg Fried Rice (see page 30) or wok-fried greens, to serve

I love to celebrate Easter with family and friends, as cooking for them is a great source of pleasure. But when you are entertaining, you want your food to be fuss free yet delicious. So I like to make my pan-fried soy butter lamb chops; they're so easy to cook and full of flavour. The light soy sauce delivers the perfect umami savoury note to complement the flavour of the lamb.

Season the lamb chops with the salt and ground black pepper.

Heat a wok or large pan over a medium heat. Place the lamb chops in the wok or pan with the fat side facing down. After rendering the fat for 4–5 minutes, add the rapeseed oil or olive oil and cook the lamb chops for 2 minutes until the meat is browned and the fat is cooked. Turn them over, then cook for another 1 minute for rare, 2 minutes for medium, and 3 minutes for medium–well done (depending on the thickness of your lamb chops).

A minute before the lamb chops are cooked, add the garlic and spring onions and cook for 10 seconds to infuse their flavour. Add the butter and heat until melted and just coating the lamb chops. Then drizzle with the light soy sauce at the end for an umami pop of flavour. Serve with Egg Fried Rice or wok-fried greens of your choice.

10 mins 5 mins

Spicy Cumin Lamb

Serves 2

For the spice rub

¼ tsp ground cumin

¼ tsp fennel seeds

¼ tsp dried chilli flakes

pinch of salt

pinch of ground black pepper

For the lamb

400g (14oz) boneless lamb loin,
cut into 1cm (½in) slices

1 tbsp cornflour

2 tbsp rapeseed oil

2 garlic cloves, finely chopped

1 red chilli, deseeded
and finely chopped

1 large white onion, sliced into
crescent slices

250g (9oz) green peppers, cored,
deseeded and cut into strips

1 tbsp Shaohsing rice wine

1 tsp dark soy sauce

1 tbsp low-sodium light soy sauce

3 tbsp cornflour

2 tbsp cold water

dash of chilli oil

fresh coriander leaves, to serve

cooked jasmine rice
(see page 22), to serve

This is a beautiful wok-fried spiced lamb dish with garlic, red chilli, onions and crunchy green peppers – it's super delicious and quick. I first had this dish in Xian. On the streets in the Muslim quarter, there were rows of stalls lined up making these appetizing lamb skewers covered in cumin, fennel, dried chilli flakes and salt. The spiced, moreish flavours and tantalising aromas are the inspiration behind this dish. You could throw in some egg noodles and turn this into a spicy lamb chow mein.

In a bowl, add all the spice rub ingredients and the lamb. Toss to coat well. Dust with the cornflour.

Heat a wok over a high heat until smoking. Add 1 tablespoon of the rapeseed oil and give it a swirl. Add the garlic, red chilli and white onion and toss for 10 seconds.

Add the remaining tablespoon of rapeseed oil. Add the lamb and let it sear on one side for 30 seconds before you flip it. Stir-fry for 20 seconds for medium.

Add the green pepper and toss together for 15 seconds to soften the peppers.

Season with the Shaohsing rice wine, dark soy sauce and light soy sauce. Mix the cornflour and water to make a slurry and pour in to thicken the sauce, tossing to coat. Add a dash of chilli oil. Garnish with coriander and serve immediately with jasmine rice.

 Vegan Option   Use chunks of smoked or fried tofu instead of the lamb

Wok For Less

5 mins

5 mins

Spicy Cumin Lamb & Pea Fried Rice

Serves 2

2 tbsp rapeseed oil

3 eggs, beaten

70g (2½oz) frozen peas

300g (10½oz) cooked jasmine rice (see page 22)

100g (3½oz) Spicy Cumin Lamb (see page 156)

1 tsp dark soy sauce

1–2 tbsp low-sodium light soy sauce

1 tbsp toasted sesame oil

pinch of ground white pepper

1 spring onion, trimmed and finely sliced on the angle, to garnish

You'll need about a handful of leftovers from the Spicy Cumin Lamb recipe (see page 156), then all you need to do is just fry them in a wok with eggs, frozen peas and leftover cooked jasmine rice for this quick and easy supper.

Heat a wok over a high heat. Add 1 tablespoon of the rapeseed oil and give it a swirl. Tip the beaten eggs into the wok, then scramble, stirring, for 1–2 minutes until fluffy. Remove and set aside.

Return the wok to the heat and add the remaining tablespoon of rapeseed oil. Let it heat up for 20 seconds, then add the frozen peas and stir-fry for less than a minute.

Add the cooked jasmine rice and, using a wooden spoon or metal spatula, start to gently break apart the rice grains: not in a stabbing motion but just tossing the ingredients well for 1–2 minutes.

Add the leftover lamb pieces and toss together for 1 minute. Add the scrambled egg back into the wok and stir through. Season with the dark soy sauce, light soy sauce, toasted sesame oil and a pinch of ground white pepper. Garnish with the spring onion and serve immediately.

5.

Easy Freezy

5 Easy Freezy

Use your freezer to make delicious meals on a budget in this chapter featuring freezables like dumplings, fish balls and meatballs that are handy to have for emergency suppers. There's initial effort involved, but once all the items are made, it's super easy. There's my Pan-Fried Chicken & Prawn Potsticker Dumplings (see page 171); Pork & Prawn, Mushroom & Bamboo Shoot Siu Mai (see page 172); Vegan Smoked Tofu Dumplings in a Savoury Broth (see page 164); Sesame Fishy Pork Squid 'Balls' (see page 166); Fish Ball Noodle Soup (see page 167); Shanghainese Lionhead Pork Meatball Noodle Soup (see page 175); Mixed Seafood Ball Noodle Soup (see page 168); and Beef Ball Udon Noodle Soup (see opposite). All the meatballs are super versatile: throw them in Chinese curry sauce or spicy Sichuan sauce and you can turn them into new delicious and flavourful meals in half the time. Double the quantities easily and follow the freezing guidelines to get extra meals on the table in minutes.

15 mins · 10 mins

Beef Ball Udon Noodle Soup

Makes 12 balls • Serves 2

For the coriander fish balls

50g (1¾oz) squid, cleaned and minced

200g (7oz) beef fillet, finely diced

pinch of sea salt flakes

pinch of ground white pepper

1 tsp Shaohsing rice wine or dry sherry

1 tbsp cornflour

1 large egg white

1 tsp oyster sauce

1 tbsp finely sliced fresh coriander stems

For the broth

1.5 litres (2¾ pints) fresh beef stock

200g (7oz) Chinese leaf, cut into 2.5cm (1in) slices

200g (7oz) cooked egg or chunky udon noodles

pinch of sea salt flakes

pinch of ground white pepper

½ tsp ground turmeric

1 tsp chilli bean sauce

1 tbsp vegetable bouillon powder

1 tbsp low-sodium light soy sauce

1 tsp chilli oil

To serve

¼ tsp chilli oil

fresh coriander leaves

a sprinkle of finely chopped chives

This is inspired by the traditional street-food eateries in Hong Kong where fresh beef balls are dipped in a curry or spicy broth and served on a stick. They are super moreish. The squid adds a naturally sweet 'chewiness' to the beef balls. If you want to freeze these, just make the balls, freeze them raw or cooked, then drop them into a hot spicy broth, or add them to an udon noodle curry soup.

Place the squid and beef in a food processor, season with salt and ground white pepper, then add the Shaohsing rice wine or sherry, cornflour, egg white and oyster sauce. Blend well until airy and light. Sprinkle over the finely chopped coriander stems and mix well.

Using 2 tablespoons, take a spoonful of the mixture and pass between both spoons, turning and smoothing the sides to shape into quenelles (pointed oval spheres). It should make 12.

Fill a large stock pot with the stock and bring to a simmer over a high heat. Add the Chinese leaf and cook for 1 minute. Add the cooked egg or udon noodles. Season with the sea salt and ground white pepper.

Turn down the heat to medium and gently add the beef balls. Cook for 2–3 minutes until the beef balls float to the surface.

Add the ground turmeric, chilli bean sauce, vegetable bouillon powder, light soy sauce and chilli oil and bring to the boil.

Divide the noodles between 2 bowls, ladle over the stock and Chinese leaf, then place 6 balls into each bowl. Drizzle over the chilli oil and sprinkle over the coriander leaves and finely chopped chives. Serve immediately.

The beef balls can be frozen raw or after cooking. To freeze, place in an airtight freezer-proof container and freeze. To cook, steam or boil the raw or cooked balls from frozen. If using raw balls, add to noodle soups or broths to cook through.

30 mins · 15 mins

Vegan Smoked Tofu Dumplings in a Savoury Broth

Makes 20 dumplings • Serves 2 or 4 to share

60g (2¼oz) long-stem broccoli stems, finely chopped

2.5cm (1in) piece of fresh root ginger, peeled and finely grated

1 spring onion, trimmed and finely chopped

50g (1¾oz) smoked tofu, cubed

40g (1½oz) firm tofu, mashed up

1 tbsp mushroom sauce

20 sheets of dumpling wrappers

For the seasoning

¼ tsp salt

¼ cube vegetable stock, grated

¼ tsp caster sugar

¼ tsp ground white pepper

½ tsp toasted sesame oil

For the hot and sour broth

1 litre (1¾ pints) vegetable stock

100g (3½oz) oyster or shimeji mushrooms, or mushroom of your choice

50 French beans, sliced on the deep angle

1 tbsp rice vinegar

2 tbsp low-sodium light soy sauce

1 tsp dark soy sauce

2 pinches of ground white pepper

½ red chilli, sliced

To garnish

1 spring onion, trimmed and sliced

1 red chilli, cut into long thin julienne pieces

fresh coriander leaves

These vegan dumplings offer an umami hit of deliciousness. The trick is marinating the tofu in the mushroom sauce for a richer flavour.

In a bowl, thoroughly mix the broccoli stem, grated ginger and spring onion with both types of tofu. Add the mushroom sauce and all of the seasoning ingredients and mix well.

Place a dumpling wrapper between your palm and fingers. Put 2 generous teaspoons of the vegetable mixture in the middle of the wrapper and fold in half. Dip your finger in water and wet all around the edges of the dumpling. Press to seal the edges together. To make the dumpling more decorative, fold the ends. Repeat until you have 20 dumplings.

Heat a wok or pan and add the vegetable stock, mushrooms, French beans, rice vinegar, light soy sauce, dark soy sauce, ground white pepper and sliced red chilli and bring to the boil. Leave to simmer while you cook the dumplings.

Bring a separate pan of water to the boil, then gently drop in the dumplings. Cook the dumplings, stirring occasionally to prevent sticking, until they all float to the surface; this should take about 2–3 minutes. Remove the dumplings from the pan using a slotted spoon and transfer to soup serving bowls. (At this point the dumplings are ready to eat; they are known as 'water-cooked', or 'shui jiao', and you can just serve them with your favourite dipping sauce – see page 192 – if you don't wish to serve them with a broth.)

Ladle over the hot and sour broth to cover the dumplings. Garnish with the spring onion, red chilli and coriander and serve immediately.

The dumplings can be frozen raw or after cooking. Place in an airtight freezer-proof container and freeze. To cook, steam or boil the raw or cooked dumplings from frozen. If using raw dumplings, add to noodle soups or broths to cook through.

10 mins

3–4 mins

Sesame Fishy Pork Squid Balls

Makes about 12 balls

For the fishy pork squid balls

100g (3½oz) lean minced pork

50g (1¾oz) squid, cleaned and diced

120g (4¼oz) halibut, finely minced or finely chopped

pinch of sea salt

pinch of ground white pepper

1 large egg white

1 tbsp oyster sauce

1 tsp toasted sesame oil

1 spring onion, trimmed and finely chopped

1 tbsp cornflour

200ml (7fl oz) rapeseed oil, for frying

To serve

toasted black sesame seeds

1 tbsp finely chopped chives

Easy Aromatic Dumpling Dipping Sauce (see page 192)

cooked jasmine rice (see page 22)

Chinese cucumber pickles

mixed salad leaves

These sesame seed-encrusted fishy pork squid balls are super easy to make and delicious. Serve them with pickles, rice and salad for a delicious Chinese-inspired poke bowl. If freezing the balls for a handy supper, do so after cooking.

In a large bowl, mix together the lean minced pork, squid and minced halibut. Add all the remaining ingredients down to the cornflour, transfer to a food processor and blend well.

Using 2 tablespoons, take a spoonful of the mixture and pass between both spoons, turning and smoothing the sides to shape into quenelles (pointed oval spheres). It should make roughly 12 mini balls.

Heat a wok or shallow pan over a medium heat. Add enough rapeseed oil to fill 2.5cm (1in) of the pan, and heat to 180°C (350°F) on a meat thermometer. The oil is hot enough when a cube of bread turns golden brown in 15 seconds.

Working in batches, gently and carefully place the balls into the hot oil. Fry until the fishy pork balls are cooked through; this should take about 2 minutes. Removed with a slotted spoon and drain on kitchen paper. Repeat until all the balls are cooked.

To serve, roll the balls in some toasted sesame seeds and finely chopped chives. Serve with your favourite dipping sauce, alongside some jasmine rice, pickles and salad leaves.

The squid balls can be frozen raw or after cooking. To freeze, place in an airtight freezer-proof container and freeze. To cook, steam or boil the raw or cooked balls from frozen. If using raw balls, add to noodle soups or broths to cook through.

15 mins 10 mins

Fish Ball Noodle Soup

Makes 12 balls

For the coriander fish balls

200g (7oz) skinned whole
haddock fillet, finely chopped

50g (1¾oz) squid, cleaned
and minced

pinch of sea salt flakes

pinch of ground white pepper

1 tsp Shaohsing rice wine
or dry sherry

1 tbsp cornflour

1 large egg white

1 tsp oyster sauce

1 tbsp finely sliced fresh
coriander stems

For the broth

1.5 litres (2¾ pints) fresh fish stock

200g (7oz) Chinese leaf,
cut into 2.5cm (1in) slices

200g (7oz) cooked vermicelli
rice noodles

pinch of sea salt flakes

pinch of ground white pepper

1 tbsp low-sodium light soy sauce

1 tsp toasted sesame oil

To serve

1 tsp chilli oil

fresh coriander leaves

1 tbsp finely chopped chives

This is inspired by the fish ball noodle shops in Hong Kong, one of my favourite places to eat. Delicious and so pure. The squid helps to add a 'bite' and natural chewiness. You can make the balls, freeze them raw or cooked, then drop them into a hot pot or noodle soup broth for a healthy emergency supper. Enjoy!

Place the haddock and squid in a food processor, season with salt and ground white pepper, then add the Shaohsing rice wine or sherry, cornflour, egg white and oyster sauce. Blend well until airy and light. Sprinkle over the finely chopped coriander stems and mix well.

Using 2 tablespoons, take a spoonful of the mixture and pass between both spoons, turning and smoothing the sides to shape into quenelles (pointed oval spheres). It should make 12.

Fill a large stock pot with the fish stock and bring to a simmer over a high heat. Add the Chinese leaf and cook for 1 minute. Add the cooked vermicelli rice noodles. Season with sea salt and ground white pepper.

Turn the heat down to medium and gently add the fish balls. Cook for 2–3 minutes until the fish balls float to the surface and turn opaque white.

Season with the light soy sauce and toasted sesame oil and bring to the boil.

Divide the noodles into 2 bowls, ladle over the stock and Chinese leaf, then place 6 fish balls in each bowl. Drizzle over the chilli oil and sprinkle over the coriander leaves and finely chopped chives. Serve immediately.

The squid balls can be frozen raw or after cooking. To freeze, place in an airtight freezer-proof container and freeze. To cook, steam or boil the raw or cooked balls from frozen. If using raw balls, add to noodle soups or broths to cook through.

15 mins

10 mins

Mixed Seafood Ball Noodle Soup

Makes 12 balls • Serves 2

For the mixed seafood balls

50g (1¾oz) tiger prawns, shelled and deveined

50g (1¾oz) squid, cleaned and minced

150g (5½oz) skinned whole haddock fillet, finely chopped

pinch of sea salt flakes

pinch of ground white pepper

1 tsp Shaohsing rice wine or dry sherry

1 tbsp cornflour

1 large egg white

1 tsp oyster sauce

1 tbsp finely sliced fresh coriander stems

For the broth

1.5 litres (2¾ pints) fresh fish stock

200g (7oz) Chinese leaf, cut into 2.5cm (1in) slices

200g (7oz) cooked vermicelli rice noodles

pinch of sea salt flakes

pinch of ground white pepper

1 tbsp low-sodium light soy sauce

1 tsp toasted sesame oil

To serve

1 tsp chilli oil

fresh coriander leaves

1 tbsp finely chopped chives

The seafood is a mix of fresh tiger prawns, squid and any white fleshed fish – I love haddock. Make the balls, freeze them raw or cooked, then drop them into a spicy hot pot or ramen noodle soup broth for a healthy speedy supper. Enjoy!

Place the tiger prawns, squid and haddock in a food processor, season with salt and ground white pepper, then add the Shaohsing rice wine or sherry, cornflour, egg white and oyster sauce. Blend well until airy and light. Sprinkle over the finely chopped coriander stems and mix well.

Using 2 tablespoons, take a spoonful of the mixture and pass between both spoons, turning and smoothing the sides to shape into quenelles (pointed oval spheres). It should make 12.

Fill a large stock pot with the fish stock and bring to a simmer over a high heat. Add the Chinese leaf and cook for 1 minute. Add the cooked vermicelli rice noodles. Season with sea salt and ground white pepper.

Turn down the heat to medium and gently add the mixed seafood balls. Cook for 2–3 minutes until the fish balls float to the surface and turn opaque white.

Season with the light soy sauce and toasted sesame oil and bring to the boil.

Divide the noodles between 2 bowls, ladle over the stock and Chinese leaf, then place 6 balls into each bowl. Drizzle over the chilli oil and sprinkle over the coriander leaves and finely chopped chives. Serve immediately.

15 mins

4-6 mins

Pan-Fried Chicken & Prawn Potsticker Dumplings

Makes 10 dumplings

250g (9oz) boneless chicken thighs, finely minced

100g (3½oz) tiger prawns, shelled, deveined and finely chopped

30g (1oz) canned water chestnuts, drained and finely chopped

2 spring onions, trimmed and finely chopped

½ tsp low-sodium light soy sauce

1 tsp oyster sauce

1 tsp toasted sesame oil

1 tsp Shaohsing rice wine

1 tsp caster sugar

2.5cm (1in) piece of fresh root ginger, peeled and finely grated

pinch of ground white pepper

1-2 tsp cornflour

10 frozen wheat-flour gyoza dumpling wrappers, defrosted

2 tbsp rapeseed oil, for frying

chilli oil or low-sodium light soy sauce, to serve

These are great to have in your freezer for an emergency dinner; just double the quantities and freeze them. I love this combination of flavours from the chicken, prawns and crunchy water chestnuts. Serve them with my Aromatic Dumpling Dipping Sauce on page 192 to give them an umami tang.

In a bowl, combine all the ingredients except the dumpling wrappers and rapeseed oil, adding just enough cornflour to hold the mixture together.

Make one dumpling at a time and keep the rest of the mixture covered with clingfilm or a damp kitchen towel.

Take a gyoza wrapper in the palm of one hand. Spoon a teaspoon of the dumpling filling in the centre and spread it out slightly. Dip a finger in some cold water and spread the water around the edges of the dumpling (this will help it seal better). Fold the wrapper in half, then with your thumb and second finger pinch to seal the dumpling, working your way around the whole dumpling. Ensure it is tightly sealed. Repeat until you have 10 dumplings.

Heat a wok or non-stick pan with a lid over a medium heat. Add the rapeseed oil and give it a swirl so it evenly coats the pan. Add the potsticker dumplings and pan-fry for 1-2 minutes. Then add just enough water to cover one-third of the dumplings. Put the lid on and cook for 3-4 minutes until the bottom of each dumpling is golden brown and the top is translucent, and when you test one, it is cooked all the way through. To test, place a cocktail stick through and if it slides out easily, it is cooked.

Serve immediately with a sauce of your choice.

To freeze, place in an airtight freezer-proof container and freeze. To cook, steam or boil from frozen or add to noodle soups or broths.

Pork & Prawn, Mushroom & Bamboo Shoot Siu Mai

Makes 10 dumplings • Serves 2–4

2.5cm (1in) piece of fresh root ginger, peeled and finely grated

1 large spring onion, trimmed and finely chopped

225g (8oz) can bamboo shoots, drained and diced

5 dried Chinese mushrooms, rehydrated in warm water for 20 minutes

220g (7¾oz) tiger prawns, shelled (100g/3½oz shelled weight), deveined and finely chopped

150g (5½oz) pork loin, roughly diced into 0.5cm (¼in) pieces

1 tbsp low-sodium light soy sauce

1 tsp sesame oil

1 tbsp Shaohsing rice wine or dry sherry

2 tsp cornflour

small pinch of ground white pepper

small pinch of sea salt

16 wonton egg wrappers or pastry sheets (available in Chinese supermarkets)

1 carrot, trimmed and cut into 0.5cm (¼in) slices (10 slices)

chilli oil, to serve (optional)

For the vinegar soy dressing

2 tbsp low-sodium light soy sauce

2 tbsp toasted sesame oil

2 tbsp clear rice vinegar

1 tsp finely chopped fresh coriander stems

1 tsp deseeded and finely chopped chillies

Pork and prawn in an open-wrapped wonton is famously recognized as 'siu mai', and is usually served in a bamboo basket. They are very healthy as they are steamed. Dim sum is a real Chinese tradition that developed around the period of the Silk Road and originated from the Canton province (Guangdong) in China. The first time I tried dim sum was in Hong Kong with my family when I was about 13, so whenever I make this recipe, it takes me back to then.

In a bowl, mix all the ingredients except the wonton wrappers and carrot slices well using your hands. Chill uncovered in the refrigerator for 30 minutes.

Remove the mix from the refrigerator and pour off any excess water. (Tip: using a pair chopsticks, mix the mixture in a clockwise direction until sticky to help improve the texture and bind all the flavours together. You can also use your hands.)

It's time to fill. Place 2 teaspoons of the filling in the centre of a wonton wrapper. Then gather the sides of the wonton wrapper and mould around the filling in a ball shape but leaving the centre unwrapped. Fold down any excess and using a pair of scissors cut away any excess wonton wrapper at the top: the siu mai should have a flat bottom, be open at the top, nipped at the waist, and filled to the top of the wrapper.

Place baking paper on a steamer rack, then line with the carrot slices. Place the siu mai dumplings on top, then place this rack in a wok half-filled with water. Place the wok lid on top, bring the water to the boil and steam over a medium–high heat for about 10–12 minutes until cooked through.

Meanwhile, mix together the vinegar soy dressing ingredients.

When the dumplings are ready, serve with the vinegar soy dressing and chilli oil, if using. The dumplings can be frozen raw before cooking or after cooking, to freeze, place in an airtight freezer-proof container and freeze. To cook, steam or boil from raw/cooked frozen add to noodle soups or broths and cook through.

15 mins

30 mins

Shanghainese Lionhead Pork Meatball Noodle Soup

Makes 6 small meatballs • Serves 2 or 4 to share

For the meatballs

500g (1lb 2oz) lean minced pork

4 garlic cloves, finely minced

5cm (2in) piece of fresh root ginger, peeled and finely grated

2 spring onions, trimmed and finely chopped

½ tsp salt

pinch of ground white pepper

50ml (2fl oz) Shaohsing rice wine or dry sherry

1 tbsp dark soy sauce

2 tbsp low-sodium light soy sauce

1 tbsp toasted sesame oil

1 egg, beaten

1 tbsp cornflour

100ml (3½fl oz) rapeseed oil, for frying

For the soup

500ml (18fl oz) vegetable stock

500ml (18fl oz) filtered water

5 dried Chinese mushrooms, sliced

200g (7oz) Chinese leaf, quartered lengthways

1 tbsp low-sodium light soy sauce

100g (3½oz) vermicelli rice noodles (add more if preferred)

1 tbsp toasted sesame oil

pinch of sea salt flakes

pinch of ground white pepper

chill oil, to serve

These mini lionhead meatballs are based on the Shanghainese dish, where tender pork meatballs are cooked with Chinese leaf, the meatballs resembling the 'mane' of the lion, while the meatballs resemble the 'lion's head'. Inspired by the classic, I've decided to make these, that are delicious in a noodle soup – simple and moreish, they're perfect for a mid-week supper. You can pre-cook and freeze all the meatballs and then add them to noodle soups or braise in some red cooking sauce 'hong sao' by boiling soy sauce, sugar, star anise, and serve with rice and pak choy – delicious.

Place all the ingredients for the meatballs except the rapeseed oil into a large bowl and stir to combine well. With wetted hands, take a medium golf ball-sized mound of mixture and roll into a round shape. Place on a plate and repeat until all you have about 6 meatballs.

Pour the rapeseed oil into a large wok or pan and heat over high heat to 150°C (300°F). Slowly and carefully add the meatballs into the oil and cook for 5–7 minutes until golden brown. Place a skewer through a meatball and if it lifts out clean, it's cooked. Lift the meatballs out of the oil and set aside.

Pour the oil from the pan into a heatproof bowl, then add 1 tablespoon back into the pan. Add the vegetable stock, measured water, Chinese mushrooms, Chinese leaf and soy sauce and cook over a medium heat for 15 minutes. Add the rice noodles and cook for a further 5 minutes. Season with toasted sesame oil, salt and ground white pepper.

Ladle into soup bowls, spoon in the meatballs and serve immediately with chilli oil.

The meatballs can be frozen after cooking. To freeze, place in an airtight freezer-proof container and freeze. To cook, steam or boil from frozen, add to noodle soups or broths.

6.

Easy Salads, Pickles & Sides

6   Easy salads, pickles & sides

This section is dedicated to some fresh side pickles, salads and veggie stir-fries that you can quickly whip up to accompany any of the meals in the book to get your ten a day. Nutritional health experts suggest we should aim to have as many different types of fresh produce each week to help maintain a healthy gut microbiome. There's my Easy Garlic or Ginger Pak Choy (see page 180); Sesame Slaw (see page 182); Miso Mangetout & Sugar Snap Peas (see page 184); French Beans in Garlic Rice Vinegar Dressing (see page 182); Smacked Garlic Cucumber Salad (see page 183); Sweetheart Cabbage with Sweetcorn & Chilli (see page 185); and Cauliflower, Pickled Ginger & Edamame Quick 'Pickle' (see page 186).

5 mins   2 mins

Easy Garlic
or Ginger Pak Choy

Serves 2

1 tbsp rapeseed oil

2 garlic cloves, finely chopped,
or 1 tsp peeled and finely
grated ginger

1 red chilli, deseeded
and finely chopped

200g (7oz) mini pak choy,
quartered lengthways

1 tbsp Shaohsing rice wine

1 tbsp low-sodium light soy sauce

1 tsp cornflour, blended
with 1 tbsp cold water

dash of toasted sesame oil

This is a great addition to any main.

Heat a wok or pan over a high heat until smoking. Add the rapeseed oil and give it a swirl. Add the garlic or ginger and chilli and stir-fry for a few seconds, then add the mini pak choy and toss for 5 seconds. Season with the Shaohsing rice wine and stir-fry for less than 1 minute.

Season with the light soy sauce, then add the cornflour slurry. Take off the heat and season with a dash of toasted sesame oil. Serve immediately.

Sesame Slaw

Serves 2–4 to share

1 tbsp tahini

1 tbsp low-sodium light soy sauce

1 tsp runny honey

1 tbsp rice vinegar

juice of ½ lime

100g (3½oz) (about 2) carrots, trimmed and finely cut into julienne strips

100g (3½oz) red cabbage, finely cut into julienne strips

100g (3½oz) white cabbage, finely cut into julienne strips

½ red onion, finely cut into julienne strips

1 spring onion, trimmed and finely chopped

5g (⅛oz) chive, finely chopped

This is great for a summer occasion and all through the warmer months. For best results, chill the sliced slaw ingredients in the refrigerator so that the slaw is nice and cold when you come to assemble it.

To make the slaw, in a bowl mix the tahini, light soy sauce, runny honey, rice vinegar and lime juice. Stir to combine the dressing.

In a separate bowl, toss together the julienned carrots, red and white cabbage, red onion and spring onion, then pour over the dressing. Squeeze over the lime juice. Garnish with the chives and set aside.

French Beans in Garlic Rice Vinegar Dressing

Serves 2

100g (3½oz) French beans, trimmed

cracked sea salt

For the dressing

1 garlic clove, minced

1 tbsp olive oil

1 tbsp clear rice vinegar

pinch of cracked sea salt

pinch of ground black pepper

I love this flavourful dish, the French beans add crunchy texture and the simple dressing is not only healthy but full of goodness. Delicious served as an accompaniment to other dishes or on plain rice.

Bring a small pan of water to the boil. Add a pinch of cracked sea salt. Add the French beans and blanch for 2 minutes. Take out and plunge in cold running water.

In a bowl, mix together the dressing ingredients. Add all the beans and toss together, then serve immediately.

Radish, Cucumber & Cherry Tomato Quick 'Pickle'

Serves 2

5 mins

6 red radishes, halved

½ cucumber, deseeded and cut into 1cm (½in) half-moons

8 cherry tomatoes, halved

2 tbsp clear rice vinegar

1 tsp low-sodium light soy sauce

1 tsp toasted sesame oil

1 tsp black sesame seeds

This delicious, quick and easy pickle is full of flavour and great with so many dishes.

Toss all the ingredients together and serve immediately.

Smacked Garlic Cucumber Salad

Serves 4 to share

5 mins
+ 15 mins
chilling

1 cucumber, smacked using the back of a cleaver, halved lengthways and sliced into 2.5cm (1in) chunks on the diagonal

For the dressing

2 garlic cloves, finely minced

2 tbsp low-sodium light soy sauce

2 tbsp rice vinegar

2 tbsp toasted sesame oil

1 tbsp mirin

1 tbsp chilli oil

1 tsp caster sugar

My classic smacked garlic cucumber salad is delicious with everything from roasted meats to noodle dishes or as a starter to whet the appetite.

When you have prepared the cucumber, chill in the refrigerator for 15 minutes.

   Just before serving, mix together the dressing ingredients in a bowl. Toss the cucumber in the dressing and serve in small bowls to share.

8 mins

3–4 mins

Miso Mangetout Sugar Snap Peas

Serves 2

1 tbsp rapeseed oil

2.5cm (1in) piece of fresh root ginger, peeled and finely grated

150g (5½oz) sugar snap peas

150g (5½oz) mangetout, halved if large

2 tbsp roasted, unsalted cashew nuts

1 tsp miso

1 tsp low-sodium light soy sauce

pinch of light brown sugar

I love the crunchy sugar snap and mangetout in this speedy stir-fry, the cashews add nuttiness and the miso is full of goodness and umami. Quick and healthy, this is a good recipe to have up your sleeve.

Heat a wok over a high heat until smoking. Add the rapeseed oil and give it a swirl. Add the ginger and allow to sizzle for 30 seconds before adding the sugar snap peas and mangetout. Stir-fry for 1–2 minutes.

Add the rest of the ingredients and toss the wok for another minute. Serve immediately.

Sweetheart Cabbage with Sweetcorn & Chilli

Serves 2

1 tbsp cornflour

2 tbsp cold water

1 tbsp rapeseed oil

2 garlic cloves, finely chopped

2.5cm (1in) piece of fresh root ginger, peeled and finely chopped

1 red chilli, deseeded and finely chopped

200g (7oz) Chinese leaf, cut into 2cm (¾in) slices

kernels from 1 fresh corn cob or 160g (5¾oz) can of sweetcorn, drained

1 tbsp Shaohsing rice wine

60ml (4tbsp) hot vegetable stock

2 tbsp low-sodium light soy sauce

dash of toasted sesame oil

1 large spring onion, trimmed and finely sliced on the diagonal

Sweet cabbage and crunchy sweetcorn kernels marry perfectly with chilli and soy to make a quick and delicious side dish.

In a cup or small bowl, mix the cornflour with the measured water to make a slurry. Set aside until needed.

Heat a wok over a high heat. Add the rapeseed oil and give it a swirl around the wok. Add the garlic, ginger and chilli and stir-fry for a few seconds, then add the Chinese leaf and the corn kernels, and cook for 2–3 minutes. Season with the Shaohsing rice wine.

Stir in the vegetable stock and light soy sauce. After 30 seconds, once the vegetables are softened but still al dente, add the cornflour slurry and toss together well to coat the vegetables.

Season with a dash of toasted sesame oil and sprinkle over the spring onion, then serve immediately.

Cauliflower, Pickled Ginger & Edamame Quick 'Pickle'

Serves 2

100g (3½oz) frozen edamame, defrosted

100g (3½oz) cauliflower, thinly sliced

1 tbsp pickled sushi ginger, finely sliced

1 tbsp mirin

1 tbsp clear rice vinegar

pinch of caster sugar

1 spring onion, trimmed and sliced, to garnish

I love the combination of sweet cauliflower, fiery sushi ginger, crunchy edamame and the bite of spring onions in this delicious and easy pickle.

In a pan, bring some water to a simmer, add the edamame beans, cook for 1 minute, drain, rinse under cold water to stop cooking and set aside.

In a bowl, mix the cauliflower, pickled sushi ginger and cooked edamame beans together and toss well. Season with the mirin, rice vinegar and pinch of caster sugar. Garnish with spring onions. Serve immediately.

Woodear Mushrooms in Chilli Soy Sesame Dressing

Serves 4

50g (1¾oz) Chinese black woodear mushrooms

2 tbsp low-sodium light soy sauce

2 tbsp toasted sesame oil

2 tbsp clear rice vinegar

1 small handful of fresh coriander, very finely chopped

1 tsp chilli oil

1 bird's eye chilli, finely sliced (very hot, so optional)

Woodear is a traditional Chinese fungus that is super healthy and has a crunchy texture. If you can't get it, use drained canned bamboo shoots instead, or any crunchy veggies like French beans, blanched broccoli and canned sweetcorn kernels will do.

Soak the woodear mushrooms in warm water for 20 minutes. Drain, then finely slice.

Place in a bowl with the light soy sauce, toasted sesame oil and rice vinegar and chill in the fridge for 15 minutes.

Add the finely chopped coriander and toss, then drizzle with the chilli oil and garnish with the finely sliced bird's eye chilli, if using.

10 mins

Sichuan-Inspired 'Guaiwei' 'Strange Flavour' Vegetable Pickles in Chilli Oil

Serves 4

4 kohlrabis, cut into 1cm (½in) cubes or wedges

6 red radishes, each cut into 6 wedges

1 carrot, trimmed and sliced into 0.5–2.5cm (¼–1in) rounds

2 tbsp mirin

For the dressing

1 tbsp chilli oil

1 tbsp light soy

2 tbsp lemon juice

¼ tsp chilli bean sauce

½ tsp caster sugar

1 tbsp tahini or peanut butter

drizzle of Sichuan pepper oil or chilli oil, to serve

'Guaiwei' translates from Mandarin Chinese as 'strange flavour'. It is spicy, numbing, nutty, sweet and sour and is one of the most distinct Sichuan flavours. I love using radishes or kohrabi and carrot, just tossed in the deep, rich flavourful dressing, super more-ish and delicious. Traditionally black rice vinegar is used but I have opted for fresh lemon juice.

Dress the kohlrabis, red radishes and carrot with the mirin, then leave to marinate in the refrigerator until ready to serve.

Just before serving mix together the dressing ingredients. Add the veggies, then toss together. Drizzle over the Sichuan pepper oil or chilli oil and serve.

7.

Serving
Sauces

7 Serving sauces

These are my go-to staples: my Easy Aromatic Dumpling Dipping Sauce (see page 192); Spicy Umami Hot Sauce (see page 192); Cheat's Homemade Fresh Sweet Chilli Sauce (see page 193); Red Chilli, Ginger & Spring Onion Soy Salsa Verde (see opposite); Raw Green Chilli, Ginger & Spring Onion Salsa Verde (see opposite); Chilli Vinegar Dressing (see page 193); Ginger Vinegar Dressing (see page 192) and Easy Aromatic Dumpling Dipping Sauce (see page 192). You could use these sauces to accompany any of the dishes in this book to add a fresh pop of flavour.

5 mins

Red Chilli, Ginger & Spring Onion Soy Salsa Verde

Serves 2

3 tbsp rapeseed oil

2.5cm (1in) piece of fresh root ginger, peeled and finely grated

1 red chilli, deseeded and finely chopped

2 spring onions, trimmed and finely chopped

2 tbsp low-sodium light soy sauce

2 tbsp rice vinegar

1 tsp toasted sesame oil

Mix all the ingredients together in a large bowl.

6–7 mins

Raw Green Chilli, Ginger & Spring Onion Salsa Verde

Serves 2–4

4 tbsp rapeseed oil

2 pinches of sea salt

2.5cm (1in) piece of fresh root ginger, peeled and finely grated

2 spring onion, trimmed and finely chopped

2 green chillies, deseeded and finely chopped

1 tsp toasted sesame oil

Mix all the ingredients together in a large bowl.

Spicy Umami
Hot Sauce

Serves 2

1 tsp chilli bean sauce or sriracha

1 tbsp hoisin sauce

1 tbsp oyster sauce

Mix all the ingredients together in a small dipping bowl.

Ginger Vinegar
Dressing

Serves 1

1cm (½in) slice of fresh root
ginger, peeled and finely sliced
into matchsticks

1 tbsp black rice vinegar

Pour the vinegar into a bowl, add the ginger and mix together.

Easy Aromatic Dumpling
Dipping Sauce

Makes 1 large bowl to share

2 garlic cloves, finely chopped

2.5cm (1in) piece of fresh root
ginger, peeled and finely chopped

1 red chilli, deseeded
and finely chopped

2 tbsp clear rice vinegar

2 tbsp chilli oil

2 tbsp oyster sauce

2 tbsp low-sodium light soy sauce

2 tbsp toasted sesame oil

2 spring onions, trimmed
and finely chopped

1 tbsp toasted white sesame seeds

Mix all the ingredients together in a large dipping bowl.

Wok For Less

Garlic
Chilli Sauce

Serves 1–2

1 garlic clove, finely minced

1 tbsp spicy chilli sauce

Mix the garlic and chilli sauce together in a small bowl.

Cheat's Homemade Fresh
Sweet Chilli Sauce

Serves 1–2 to share

2 red chillies, deseeded

2 tbsp mirin

2 tbsp golden syrup

Put the chillies into a food processor or pestle and mortar and blend or pound until smooth. Mix together with the mirin and golden syrup in a small bowl.

Chilli Vinegar
Dressing

Serves 1

1 red chilli, finely sliced

1 tbsp black rice vinegar

Mix the chilli and vinegar together in a small bowl.

Glossary

Bamboo shoots

These add a crunchy texture to dishes. Boiled bamboo sprouts are also pickled in brine or chilli oil. Low in fat and sugar, they are a source of protein and fibre.

Beansprouts

These are crunchy and delicate, sprouted from mung beans, and a source of fibre, protein, vitamin C and folic acid.

Brown rice vinegar

This is made from unpolished brown rice and is reputedly richer in nutrients than polished rice vinegar. It is light brown in colour and is sweeter and less acidic than other vinegars. It can be found in health food stores or online.

Buckwheat/soba noodle

A Japanese noodle made from buckwheat ('soba' means 'buckwheat') and wheatflour, which gives it a dark brownish-grey color. They are medium in thickness and available in several varieties such as cha soba, made with tea leaves and buckwheat. You can find them in Asian markets, and they can be stored for 6–8 months. They make an ideal ingredient in a noodle salad. They are free from fat and cholesterol and a good source of manganese, protein, complex carbohydrates and thiamin. If 100 per cent buckwheat, they do not contain gluten.

Button mushrooms

These come in white or brown varieties and are also known as the common mushroom. They are an excellent source of B vitamins, riboflavin, niacin and pantothenic acid. They are also a good source of the mineral phosphorus.

Chilli bean paste

Made from broad beans and chillies that have been fermented with salt to give a deep brown-red sauce. Some versions include fermented soybeans or garlic. Good in soups and braised dishes; use this paste with caution, as some varieties are extremely hot.

Chilli oil

A fiery, orange-red oil made by heating dried red chillies in oil. To make your own, heat groundnut oil in a wok, add dried chilli flakes with seeds and cook for 2 minutes. Take off the heat and leave the chilli to infuse in the oil until completely cooled. Decant into a glass jar and store for a month before using. For a clear oil, pass through a sieve.

Chilli sauce/chilli garlic sauce

A bright red sauce made from chillies, vinegar, sugar and salt. Some varieties are flavoured with garlic and vinegar.

Chinese leaf/cabbage

This has a sweet aroma with a mild flavour that disappears when cooked. The white stalk has a crunchy texture and remains succulent even after prolonged cooking. It is used for kimchi.

Chinese chives (garlic chives)

These are long, flat, green leaves with a strong garlic flavour. There are two varieties; one has small yellow edible flowers at the top. Both are delicious. A good substitute is fine chives.

Chinese five spice powder

A blend of five spices – cinnamon, cloves, Sichuan peppercorns, fennel and star anise – that give the distinctive flavours of Chinese cooking.

Chinese wood ear mushrooms

A dark brown-black fungi with ear-shaped caps. Very crunchy in texture, they do not impart flavour but add colour and crispness. They should be soaked in hot water for 20 minutes before cooking – they will double in size.

Chinkiang black rice vinegar

A strong aromatic vinegar made from fermented rice. Mellow and earthy, it gives dishes a wonderful smoky flavour. Balsamic vinegar is a good substitute.

Chiu Chow chilli oil

Originating from the Chaozhou region of Southern China, this chilli oil has a unique taste and heat. Chewy and aromatic, it is made from a combination of preserved chillies in salt and garlic, soy, soybean and sesame oil.

Cinnamon stick/bark

The dried bark of various trees in the Cinnamomum genus. It can be used in pieces or ground. When ground it adds a sweet, woody fragrance.

Coconut milk

Coconut milk is the diluted cream pressed out from the thick, white flesh of a well-matured coconut. Good coconut milk has a clean, white colour and tastes rich, creamy and mildly sweet. Natural coconut cream should rise to the top and separate from the heavier water component. Coconut cream is also available in tins and used in curries and desserts. Condensed sweet coconut milk is concentrated coconut milk and sugar used in desserts as syrup. Coconut milk contains high levels of iron, calcium, potassium, magnesium, and zinc, and good amounts of vitamins C and E, rich in lauric acid and monoglyceride fats.

Courgettes

Also known as 'the little squash', these vegetables are very versatile. Choose courgettes that are unblemished and firm. They do not need to be peeled and can be eaten raw. You can use them to make spiralised courgetti 'noodles', and they are delicious roasted, stir-fried, or in soups and curries. They are packed with nutrients from Vitamins C and A, potassium, folate and fibre.

Cumin

Cumin is the pale green seed of Cuminum cyminum, a small herb in the parsley family. Cumin has a distinctive, slightly bitter yet warm flavour. Ground cumin is stronger than whole seeds. It contains magnesium and iron.

Daikon (white radish)

Resembling a large white carrot, this crunchy vegetable has a peppery taste and pungent smell, and is eaten raw, pickled or cooked. It contains vitamin C and diastase, which aids digestion. Koreans use it to make kimchi.

Dofu/fresh bean curd

Described as the 'cheese' of China, this is made from soybean curd and takes on the flavour of whatever ingredients it is cooked with. Called tofu in Japan and dofu in Chinese, it is high in protein and also contains B vitamins, isoflavones and calcium. Available as firm, soft and silken, the firm variety is great in soups, salads and stir-fries. Silken has a cream cheese-like texture. Dofu gan is dried firm smoked beancurd.

Dark soy sauce – see Soy sauce

Dried Chinese mushrooms

These need to be soaked in hot water for 20 minutes before cooking. They have a strong aroma and a slightly salty taste and complement savoury dishes.

Dried folded flat rice noodles

These are naturally gluten-free and highly versatile. They are made from a paste of rice flour and water, then steamed, formed, cut and dried. To prepare boil a litre (1¾ pints) of water and soak the noodles in it for 5–10 minutes, drain and toss through some toasted sesame oil. These are used in the popular Thai stir fry – Pad Thai.

Dried wide knife-cut noodles

Made from wheatflour, these are also known as Dao Xiao Mian from the Shanxi province in China. Also known as knife shaved or knife cut noodles. You can buy the wide dried flat versions in Chinese supermarkets. Look for those made in Taiwan, China, which are the best quality.

Edamame beans

These are harvested while the beans are still attached to their branches (eda means 'branches' and mame 'beans' in Japanese). High in protein, they are cooked whole and the seeds are then squeezed out. They are rich in complete protein, fibre, vitamins and minerals.

Enoki mushrooms

Tiny, long-stemmed mushrooms with a delicate flavour. Used raw, they add texture to salads. Lightly steamed, they are slightly chewy. They are virtually fat free, provide complex carbohydrates and are high in B vitamins. They also contain pantothenic acid, riboflavin, folate, potassium and phosphorus.

Fennel seeds

Fennel is a strong aromatic spice that has a slight aniseed flavour. Delicious when toasted or pan-fried.

Fermented salted black beans

Small black soybeans preserved in salt. Rinse in cold water before use. They are used to make black bean sauce.

Fermented yellow bean paste

Made from yellow soybeans, water and salt. A substitute would be hoisin sauce, though this is sweeter and not as salty.

Hoisin sauce

Made from fermented soybeans, sugar, vinegar, star anise, sesame oil and red rice, this is great used as a marinade and as a dipping sauce.

Jasmine rice

A long-grain white, silky rice originating from Thailand that has a nutty jasmine-scented aroma. Rinse before cooking until the water runs clear.

King trumpet mushrooms

Dense and spongy when raw but have a savoury umami flavour once cooked and give a soft crunchy texture. The stalks can be shredded and stir-fried, and have a mild abalone-like flavour.

Kimchi

A Korean staple made from salted and fermented Chinese cabbage mixed with Korean radish, Korean dried chilli flakes, spring onions, ginger and geotgal (salted seafood). In my vegan version, I used red miso paste instead of seafood.

Kohlrabi

A German turnip, same species as broccoli, kale, cauliflower, Brussel sprouts, cabbage and gai lan (Chinese broccoli). It can be eaten raw or cooked. When raw it is crunchy and mildly spicy. Delicious in salads, pickled or stir-fried.

Korean chilli flakes (gochugaru)

Made by drying the chillies in the sun then crushing them, these vibrant red flakes impart a spicy taste with a hint of sweetness. A good substitute is dried chilli flakes.

Korean yellow bean paste (doenjang)

Similar to Chinese yellow bean paste and Japanese Miso, this is made from fermented soy beans and brine. It is also flavoured with garlic and sesame oil and mixed with Korean chilli paste to produce samjang sauce. Miso is available in supermarkets so use miso if you cannot find Korean doenjang.

Korean chilli paste (gochujang)

A savoury, sweet, fermented paste made from Korean red chilli powder, glutinous rice, and salt-and-barley malt powder. Soybeans are also sometimes used.

Lemongrass (citronella root)

A tough, lemon-scented stalk popular in Thai and Vietnamese cuisines. Look for lemon-green stalks that are tightly formed, firm and heavy with no bruising, tapering to a deeper green.

Minced soy

Minced soy is made from soy flour and contains soy proteins. It is a healthy economic meat substitute and includes complete proteins which means it contains all the essential amino acids. Minced soy can be dried or ground in flakes. To prepare it, pour over hot boiled water and leave to rehydrate. Use in stir-fries and curries.

Mirin

A sweet Japanese rice wine similar to sake, with a lower alcohol content but more sugar (which occurs naturally as a result of the fermentation process).

Miso paste

A thick Japanese paste made from fermented rice, barley, soybeans, salt and a fungus called kojikin. Sweet, earthy, fruity and salty, it comes in many varieties depending on the types of grains used. Organic red and yellow varieties are available in most supermarkets. A complete protein, containing all the essential amino acids; a probiotic food; rich in B-complex vitamins; contains calcium, iron, zinc, copper and magnesium.

Mushroom oyster sauce – see Oyster sauce

Nori (dried seaweed)

Sold in thin sheets, this is usually roasted until it turns black or purple-green. Used as a garnish or to wrap sushi. Once opened, a pack must be stored in an airtight container or it loses its crispness. If this happens, roast the sheets over an open flame for a few seconds until crisp. A good source of calcium, iron, zinc, vitamins B12 and C and iodine.

Oyster mushrooms

Soft and chewy with a slight oyster taste, this white, yellow or grey oyster-shaped fungi is moist and fragrant.

Pad thai noodles

Flat noodles, 5mm (¼in) wide, made from rice. They need to be soaked in hot water for 5 minutes before cooking.

Pak choi

A vegetable with broad green leaves, which taper to white stalks. Crisp and crunchy, it can be boiled, steamed or stir-fried. Contains vitamin A, C and K.

Pickled sushi ginger

Also known as 'gari', this is a type of tsukemono 'Japanese' pickled vegetables. Made from thin sliced ginger, marinated in a solution of sugar and vinegar. Delicious on sushi rice.

Ramen

Noodles, invented in China, that are used in Japanese noodle soups. They come in various thicknesses and shapes, but most are made from wheatflour, salt, water and kansui (alkaline mineral water); the latter gives the noodles a yellow hue and a firmer texture.

Red miso paste – see Miso paste

Rice vinegar

A clear, mild vinegar made from fermented rice. Cider vinegar can be used as a substitute. Chinese black rice vinegar is a rich vinegar used in braised dishes and sauces, and with noodles. When cooked, it gives a smoky flavour with a mellow and earthy taste. Balsamic vinegar makes a good substitute.

Seaweed

Excellent source of iodine; rich in protein, calcium, vitamins A and B12 and omega-3 fatty acids.

Sesame seeds

These oil-rich seeds add a nutty taste and a delicate texture to dishes. Available in black, white/yellow and red varieties, toasted and untoasted.

Seasoned sushi rice vinegar

Also known as sushi vinegar. Made from rice vinegar with added salt, sugar and sake (sometimes mirin), it is ready to use to season just-cooked sushi rice. This can be bought in most supermarkets or online Asian stores.

Shaohsing rice wine

Made from rice, millet and yeast that has been aged for 3–5 years, it gives a bittersweet finish. Dry sherry makes a good substitute.

Shiitake mushrooms

These dark brown umbrella-shaped fungi are prized for their culinary and medicinal properties. The dried variety needs to be soaked in water for 20 minutes before cooking.

Shimeji (beech) mushrooms

These come in white or brown varieties, and have long stems and concave caps.

Sichuan peppercorns

Known as Hua jiao in Mandarin or 'flower pepper', these have a pungent, citrusy aroma. They can be wok-roasted, cooked in oil to flavour the oil, or mixed with salt as a condiment.

Soy sauce

Made from wheat and fermented soybeans, soy sauce is available in dark and light varieties. Dark soy sauce is aged for longer, and is mellower and less salty. Light soy sauce is used in China instead of salt. Wheat-free varieties, called tamari, are available, though salty. You can also buy low-sodium varieties.

Soybean noodles

Thin, gluten-free dried noodles that are rich in protein and low in fat. They yield about double the amount of wheat-flour noodles once rehydrated.

Sriracha chilli sauce

A hot sauce made from chilli peppers, distilled vinegar, garlic, salt and sugar. It is named after the coastal town of Si Racha, Eastern Thailand.

Smoked tofu – see Tofu

Ssamjang – see Korean yellow bean paste

Star anise

The fruit of a small evergreen plant, these are called bajio or 'eight horns' in Chinese. They have a distinct aniseed flavour and are one of the ingredients found in Chinese five spice powder.

Sweet chilli sauce

You can make your own sweet chilli sauce by boiling fresh red chillies, adding sugar and cook down, then blitz in a food processor. Store in a jar for 1 week. Shop-bought is widely available.

Tahini

Made from soaking sesame seeds in water and then crushing them to separate the bran from the kernels. The crushed seeds are soaked in salt water, causing the bran to sink. The floating kernels are skimmed off the surface and toasted and ground to make an oily rich paste. Used in Middle Eastern cuisines and in hummus.

Tamari – see Soy sauce

Tamarind sauce/paste

The tamarind tree produces a pod-like fruit. The edible pulp is tart and used across Southeast Asia in curries.

Tempeh

A nutrient-dense soy product with a nutty mushroom flavour and chunky texture. It is fermented and is high in protein, vitamins and minerals. It contains prebiotics which can help improve digestive health and reduce inflammation. It supports oxidative stress, decreases cholesterol and improves bone health. It doesn't contain salt and is delicious marinated with soy – perfect grilled, wok-fried or in curries.

Thai green curry paste

A spicy curry paste from Thailand that uses fresh green chillies blended with shallots, coriander roots, galangal, lemongrass, salt, kaffir lime leaves, Thai basil, ground white pepper. Delicious for marinading, in stir-fries or curries. If you're vegan, check the ingredients.

Thai red curry paste

A spicy curry paste that uses fresh red chillies blended with garlic, shallots, coriander roots, galangal, lemongrass, salt, kaffir lime leaves, Thai basil, ground black pepper. Delicious for marinading, or in stir-fries and curries. If you're vegan, check the ingredients.

Thai basil

Widely used throughout Southeast Asia. Thai Basil leaves are also known as sweet basil, and have small, narrow purple stems and green leaves. They have an aniseedy-liquorice flavour and are a delicious garnish to finish Thai curries and stir-fries. Can be bought from supermarkets or Asian supermarkets. If you can't find them, leave them out.

Toasted sesame oil

Made from white pressed and toasted sesame seeds, this oil is used as a seasoning and is not suitable for use as a cooking oil since it burns easily. The flavour is intense, so use sparingly.

Tofu

This is made by boiling soy milk, adding a solidifying agent such as calcium sulfate, separating out the curds, and pressing the 'cheese' solids into moulds. Sometimes called 'soy cheese', the result is a smooth, textured ingredient.

Togarashi shichimi/Shichimi pepper flakes/Japanese pepper flakes (nana-iro togarashi)

A Japanese spice salt that contains ground red chilli pepper, ground Sichuan peppercorns, roasted orange peel, white and black sesame seeds, hemp seeds, nori and ground ginger.

Turmeric

A perennial plant belonging to the ginger family, native to India and the East Indies. The powder form comes from the underground stems and is used in curries to give a yellow colour. One of the strongest anti-inflammatories and anti-oxidants, according to Chinese medicine.

Vegetarian mushroom sauce

Sometimes known as mushroom oyster sauce – a salty seasoning sauce made from cooked-down mushrooms (it does not contain oysters and is a vegetarian version of oyster sauce). Choose one that is thick and has a glossy shine.

Vegetable shortening

Usually made from palm oil. As a more healthier alternative use half olive butter and half coconut oil as a substitute.

Vegetable bouillon stock powder

A natural flavour enhancer made from dehydrated vegetable stock. Delicious in soups, stews, sauces, curries.

Vermicelli mung bean noodles – see Mung bean noodles

Vermicelli rice noodle

Similar to vermicelli mung bean noodles, they come in many different widths and varieties. Before cooking, soak in hot water for 5 minutes. For salads, soak for 20 minutes. Add them dry for soups.

Vietnamese soy sauce

Vietnamese soy sauce is also

called Tuong. There are many different varieties and some that use soybean paste. Hac xi dau in Vietnamese likens to Chinese dark soy sauce and adds a salty taste and mahogany brown colour to dishes. Substitute with Chinese dark soy sauce.

Vietnamese rice paper

Also known as banh trang, made from white rice flour, tapioca flour and salt. The tapioca flour gives the rice paper its sticky and smooth texture. Comes dried in thin, crisp, translucent sheets. Plunge each one in warm water for 10 seconds to make it pliable to make rice paper 'summer' rolls. They can be filled with different fillings and eaten raw. Cover the rolls with slightly damp kitchen paper to prevent them drying out.

Wakame seaweed

Usually comes dried and needs to be soaked in warm water for 5 minutes. Dark green in colour, it tastes of the sea and is slightly mineral in flavour. Health benefits include lowering cholesterol, decreasing blood pressure, reducing blood sugar and aiding weightloss. Add to soups and salads or braised dishes.

Water chestnuts

The roots of an aquatic plant that grows in freshwater ponds, marshes and lakes, and in slow-moving rivers and streams. Unpeeled, they resemble a chestnut and have a firm, crunchy texture.

Wasabi

The wasabi plant is a Japanese horseradish. Wasabi paste is spicy and contains mustards and green colouring.

Wheat-flour noodles

Thin, white dried noodles. Don't confuse these with thick Japanese udon noodles.

Wheat-flour pancakes (fresh)

Made from wheatflour, water and salt and rolled in very thin discs, these are steamed before serving. They can also be found in the frozen or chilled sections of Asian supermarkets.

Wheatflour dumpling skins/ wrappers

Made from salt, flour and water. These are used to make a dough that encases vegetable and meat fillings to make dumplings. Available ready made from Chinese supermarkets, frozen or fresh. When using, cover with a damp towel.

Whole dried red chillies

Hot and fragrant, these are usually sun-dried. You can grind the chillies in a pestle and mortar to give flakes.

Yellow bean sauce

Made from fermented yellow soybeans, dark brown sugar and rice wine, this is a popular ingredient in Sichuan and Hunan province in China. Yellow bean paste is thicker and is used in marinades and as a flavouring in savoury dishes.

Index

UK/US Glossary

Ingredients

aubergine: eggplant

bicarbonate of soda: baking soda

caster sugar: superfine sugar

caster sugar: superfine sugar

chestnut mushrooms: cremini mushrooms

chickpeas: garbanzo beans

Chinese leaf: nappa cabbage/ Chinese cabbage

clingfilm: plastic wrap

cocktail stick: toothpick

coriander (fresh): cilantro

cornflour: corn starch

courgette: zucchini

eggs: These are all medium (US large) unless stated otherwise. Note that "large" eggs in this book are equivalent to US extra-large.

French beans: string beans/green beans

golden syrup: can substitute corn syrup

groundnut oil: peanut oil

long-stem broccoli: broccolini

mangetout: snow peas

minced (meat): ground

pak choi: bok choy

pepper (red/green/yellow): bell pepper

plain flour: all-purpose flour

pork belly: pork side

prawns: shrimp

rapeseed oil: canola oil

rasher (bacon): slice

spring onion: scallion

stock: broth

Equipment

baking paper: parchment paper

casserole dish: Dutch oven

frying pan: skillet

griddle pan: grill pan

grill: broiler

kitchen foil: aluminum foil

kitchen paper: paper towels

roasting tray: roasting pan

sieve: fine mesh strainer

tea towel: dish towel

Wok For Less

Acknowledgements

A big thank you to my publisher Joanna Copestick, my editorial director Judith Hannam for making 'Wok For Less' a reality and creating another stunning book. Thank you for sharing in my vision, your support means the world to me. Thank you to my manager Kate Heather RHTalent for your continued belief, deep support, strength and friendship over the years.

Thank you to the wider team at Kyle Books - to Editorial Assistant Emma Hanson, for your attention to detail and for pulling it all together so beautifully. Thank you to Evi-O. Studio – Katherine Zhang and Emi Chiba for the funky design of the book that is a gorgeous addition to the others. With thanks to the incredibly talented Jamie Cho for the photography – I loved wokking together on this one with you, and love the stunning imagery. With thanks to Emily Noto for your hard work on the production of the book.

This book is for all my fans – you wokstars - who have continued to follow and support me on my cooking journey. Do you know it has been a 20-year journey! I am forever grateful for your love and support to those who have been along for the ride. Truly I am humbled and indebted. I hope that despite the current dark clouds circulating the economy, that this book will help blow away some of that, so that you find joy and comfort in the recipes. I hope that you will glean new ideas and tips, whether you are a meat lover or veggie person, I hope there is something here for you and your loved ones. Writing this book was a labour of love, I pushed myself to cook and food style every single dish, it's not all perfect, but in the challenge, I found joy. Cooking is a process, it's in the practice that we become good and then better, as long as we keep trying. Our beauty is in our potentiality, so never give up. Whatever journey you are on, keep creating your story and despite external or personal struggles, keep smiling and keep wokking.

I sincerely hope you love 'Wok for Less' as much as I have loved creating it. I would love to hear your feedback, please do write to me at supportchinghehuang.com or please do follow me on www.chinghehuang.com Facebook/Instagram @chinghehuang I would love to hear how you get on.

A very special thanks to Chef Tom Kerridge for his generous words on my book cover – you wok Tom and am in awe of you and work – you are a cooking hero not just to me but to many. Thanks to all chef friends and the teams whom I have the pleasure in wokking with, in front and behind the scenes in the 'industry', your hard work, dedication and passion is inspiring, thanks for making the experiences a joy. To higher powers in telly world, thank you for continuing to give me opportunities to share my work.

To all my family and friends, near or far, you know who you all are. You are all my rock and my journey is very much yours, through all the meals we have shared together, through all the delicious memories made – your smiles, kind words, inspiration, unwavering support is deeply heartfelt. Love you all.

For my mum and dad, I'm so proud to be your daughter. In your courage to create a better life for us, immigrants to South Africa and then to U.K., you have given me love, extraordinary experiences and unforgettable lessons. I love you and am eternally grateful.

All my books are for the sets of 3 grandparents – Wu, Huang and Longhurst – and all our past ancestors before us, my angels and guiding lights, thank you for your love, inspiration and blessings.

To Jamie, my husband, I am so lucky to have you, as my no.1 photographer, but as my partner through every high and low, I could not have navigated this journey without you - you wok my world, you are my star of hearts.